D1520867

AARON LOPEZ
and
JUDAH TOURO

AARON LOPEZ

and

JUDAH TOURO

A Refugee and a Son of a Refugee

By

MORRIS A. GUTSTEIN, Ph. D.

Mori G. Gutst

BEHRMAN'S JEWISH BOOK HOUSE

Publishers   *New York*

1939

Copyright, 1939, By
MORRIS A. GUTSTEIN

PRINTED IN THE UNITED STATES OF AMERICA

DEDICATED

TO THE

CITY OF NEWPORT, RHODE ISLAND

ON ITS

TERCENTENARY

1639—1939

"THAT NOE PERSON WITHIN THE SAYD COLONYE, AT ANY TYME HEREAFTER, SHALL BEE ANY WISE MOLESTED, PUNISHED, DISQUIETED, OR CALLED IN QUESTION, FOR ANY DIFFERENCE IN OPINION IN MATTERS OF RELIGION WHICH DOE NOT ACTUALLY DISTURB THE CIVILL PEACE OF OUR SAYD COLONYE; BUT THAT ALL AND EVERYE PERSON AND PERSONS MAY, FROM TYME TO TYME, AND AT ALL TYMES HEREAFTER, FREELYE AND FULLYE HAVE AND ENJOYE HIS AND THEIRE OWNE JUDGMENTS AND CONSCIENCES, IN MATTERS OF RELIGIOUS CONCERNMENTS" (*Rhode Island Charter*)

ACKNOWLEDGMENT

The author wishes to record here his gratitude to

Saul Abrams, Esq., Providence, R. I.
Dr. Samuel Adelson, Newport, R. I.
Judge Robert M. Dannin, Newport, R. I.
Morris Espo, Esq., Pawtucket, R. I.
A. L. Greenberg, Esq., Newport, R. I.
and the General Jewish Council of Rhode Island,

who helped to make possible the publication of this book.

TABLE OF CONTENTS

ILLUSTRATIONS

PREFACE

IN THESE ESSAYS the aim has been to give a true picture of Aaron Lopez and Judah Touro and their contribution to our country. In these days of propaganda and agitation against the refugees, who are finding a haven in America, with the pretense that they increase the difficulties of our economic problems, it is well to remember that our country has been built with the energy and enterprise of immigrants and foreigners who came to this country as refugees from persecution in other lands, and who enriched this country rather than increased its economic difficulties. In these days when religious hatred is being fomented in all lands by people of all color under the cloak of patriotism and at times in religious disguise—a menace which has gripped our country as well—it is well to recall the words of Louis D. Brandeis, that "throughout the years we have admitted to our country and to citizenship immigrants from the diverse lands of Europe. We had faith that thereby we would best serve ourselves and mankind. This faith has been justified."

Aaron Lopez and Judah Touro are but two examples.

Within the scope of such a small volume it is of course impossible to give an exhaustive study of these two personalities. Because of the popularity, it is obvious that on many previous occasions parts of the lives of Lopez and Touro have been written. Therefore, some of the material in the book may not be altogether new to the reader. On the whole the author attempted to give as much new material on the subject as only possible within the scope of this work. To a great extent the writer personally examined the original manuscript material available. Where secondary sources have been used, the sources have been carefully checked and examined.

I wish at this time to record my sincere gratitude to Erich A. O'D. Taylor, Esq., of Newport, for the aid and suggestions he gave me in preparing the manuscript for publication and for translating Spanish-Portuguese documents into English for me.

MORRIS A. GUTSTEIN
Newport, R.I.
September, 1939

FOREWORD

Of the myriads who pass a lifetime in space and time very few are remembered beyond the third or fourth generation. Only a few leave their imprints on the sand of time; the greater number pass into eternal oblivion. Only a few become famous; the greater number pass away unsung.

The scientist leaves his impress because he searches out facts and studies the physical verities of the world; the theologian because he brings his fellowmen to the verities of the spiritual world. The warrior receives recognition because of the battles won amid slaughter and desolation; the statesman by his achievements in diplomacy, politics and government. The historian finds fame through the records of the past, bringing to living men pictures of events gone by; the poet is immortalized through his inspiring verse and his enchanting tales. The philosopher wins his reputation by his studies of the fundamental concepts of good and evil; the philanthropist by scattering his bounty for the benefit of mankind.

Among the many who must not be forgotten is

the merchant whose distributive genius has advanced the economic progress of the world. In the development of a new country social foresight and genius for trade and finance play the important roles, and the pioneers in industry and trade are of utmost importance.

Two such pioneers were Aaron Lopez and Judah Touro.

AARON LOPEZ

AARON LOPEZ

AARON LOPEZ

WHERE the famous Bellevue Avenue in Newport, Rhode Island, once known as "Jew's Street," begins, there is a famous cemetery. The marred inscriptions on the gray tombstones in that "Eternal Abode" enable one to conjure pictures of days gone by and of dreams dreamed once upon a time. It is here that many of "the tribe of the wandering foot and wearied breast" were laid to rest in the Peace of Eternity; of many of whom the poet sang:

> Pride and humiliation hand in hand
> > Walked with them through the world where'er
> > > they went;
> Trampled and beaten were they as the sand,
> > And yet unshaken as the continent.

The stone monuments which the elements of nature have left unharmed preserve the memory of a tale in which we meet "dignified hidalgos bearing such sun-warmed names as Rodrigues Rivera, Lopez or Touro, working, playing and praying harmoniously with their brethren from bleaker climes who bear such names as Pollock, Myers or Hart." The cold slabs and the dead letters recall to life "victims of medieval persecution, and the romance of their martyred faith hidden in the untouchable recesses of their soul until in Rhode Island's freedom the cherished faith could again be avowed in light and liberty." Some were pilgrim pioneers of Colonial days. Some were heroes of the Revolutionary days. Most were refugees from the oppression which has not ended for the Jew even in modern days.

Obscure, unnoticed and half hidden by the branches spreading shadows over the sepulchres there is a marble slab marking the resting place of one whose memory it recalls in the words:

> He was a Merchant of Eminence,
> of Polite & amiable manners.
> Hospitality, Liberality and Benevolence
> were his true Characteristicks.

It is the memorial stone of Aaron Lopez.

In a small rectangular enclosure surrounded by an iron fence there towers a granite obelisk which marks the resting place of one whose memory it recalls in the words:

> By righteousness and integrity he collected his wealth
> In charity and for salvation he dispensed it.

It is the memorial stone of Judah Touro.

This is the story of Aaron Lopez.

The history of the city of Newport—founded in 1639—concerns many persons of distinction who by their industrial and commercial enterprises con-

tributed to the growth of the colonies and to the
building of our United States of America. From the
crumbling old wharves and from the mouldering
timbers of the old buildings come memories and
tales of sloops and ships, of mirth and melancholy,
of adventure and of travels on high seas. They
conjure pictures of busy warehouses and cheerful
crowded coffeehouses of days gone by. They recall
tales of captains and sailors, merchants and sea-
farers, whalers and shipbuilders. Out of it all there
emerges a picture of a man whose commercial activity was emblematic of the great industrial and
commercial city which was Newport before the
American Revolution; a man who by virtue of his
courage and ability in commerce merited the honorable title of "Merchant Prince"—Aaron Lopez.

The commodious harbor, the luxuriance of the
foliage and the variety of the countryside of Newport attracted settlers from the very day white man
first approached it. The spirit of the settlement was
expressed by the founders in the code of laws of
1641, which defined the settlement as a "Democ-
racie" and specified that:

NONE BEE ACCOUNTED A DELINQUENT FOR
DOCTRINE: PROVIDED; IT BEE NOT DI-
RECTLY REPUGNANT TO YE GOVERNMENT
OR LAWES ESTABLISHED.

By virtue of all this the city grew rapidly. To its
shores people of all denominations were attracted.
The coming of the Jews to Newport dates from

the earliest period of its founding. An enchanting tale is associated with the arrival of the first Jewish settlers. It was during the time when the settlement was not as yet recognized as a separate colony and the Massachusetts Puritans objected to the granting of its charter. The Inquisition was still at the height of its power on the continent of Europe and in South America. Many Marranos—Neo-Christians of Jewish origin—molested by the Inquisition, frightened and insecure, left the Iberian peninsula and the other places of persecution to find homes where they would not be troubled. Every little boat, fighting the waves of the Atlantic and braving the perils of the sea, carried some of the Marrano families, who maintained strict secrecy as to their origin. Some were lost at sea; some were sold as slaves; and some fell into the hands of pirates.

At that remote period—in the middle of the seventeenth century—it is said, a Marrano family came to Newport. The name of the head of that family was Habib Ben-Em. This family lived at first for a little while in Amsterdam, Holland, where they openly confessed Judaism and were members of the Community headed by the famous Menasseh Ben Israel who, aided and encouraged by Roger Williams, successfully pleaded for the admission of the Jews to England.

They came to Newport in the Fall. Though it was six months before the Passover Festival they were greatly concerned about the observance of the holiday. Their principal desire was to obtain Mat-

zoth—unleavened bread—and a Hagadah—the
ritual book containing the order of the Service conducted at the home on the first two eves of the Passover.

Habib Ben-Em had a brother Abraham Israeli
living in Jerusalem. A sister of Habib married the
famous Inquisitor Diego de Aguilar who in an auto
da fé condemned his own sister to be burned alive
for Judaizing. Perhaps shaken by his sister's constancy, Diego determined to abandon his Christian
faith. He escaped with his mother from Spain, became converted to Judaism, and finally settled in
Vienna, the capital of Austria, where he became a
prominent figure in the court of Queen Maria
Theresa.

Habib addressed a letter to Holland in the beginning of the winter requesting the necessities for the
observance of the Passover. In this letter, Habib,
in harmony with the liberal spirit of Roger Williams, said:

> This is the place for the Jews; here in the colonies of
> North America, especially in the colony of Rhode Island
> where it is expected that every inhabitant will be able to
> erect a Temple to his God. Our family will remain here.
> We are sure more Jews will gather here, as sure as we
> are that day follows night. And as we are determined
> to remain here we must think of the future. After the
> winter comes the Passover Feast, and so we must be
> thinking about that . . . .

Habib asks that his relatives in Amsterdam re-
quest his brother in Jerusalem to provide him with

Matzoth. When the Matzoth arrived in Amsterdam from Jerusalem, a relative of Habib took
charge of them, secured a Hagadah and proceeded
to Newport.

On his arrival in Newport, Habib's relative from
Amsterdam met Doctor Rodrigues Malatesto of
Maryland, a physician who had come to Newport
in the interest of his fellow colonists. Marranos had
a secret sign—Shema Yisrael—by which they recognized one another. It was given as an indication that
they could converse freely. Doctor Malatesto, a
refugee Marrano, responded to the sign, thus iden-
tifying himself as a Jew. He joined the rest in the
first celebration of the Passover Feast in North
America. The story goes that it was at this Seder-
service that the Congregation Yeshuat Israel—Salvation of Israel—was founded.

This is said to have happened between the re-
conquest of Brazil by the Portuguese in 1654 and the
year 1658.

According to this story, those early settlers left
the colony for some reason soon after that first
Passover celebration in North America. Documentary evidence extant warrants this. For when
we hear of the Jews of Newport again, in connection with the purchase of the cemetery in which rest
the remains of Lopez and Touro, the document
records: "but if it Should So fall out that ye Jews
Should all Depart the Island Again So as that there
shall be none left."

This was in the year 1677, when the "Jews and

their Nation Society or Friends" through Mordecai
Campernell and Moses Israel Pachecho purchased
the plot of land in what was then the outskirts of
the city and now is the beginning of Bellevue Avenue, opposite a modern hotel.

Campernell who originally lived in Brazil and
Pachecho who originally lived in Hamburg came
from Barbados with the others who constituted the
nucleus of the Jewish community of Newport.

June 24, 1684, the General Assembly of Rhode
Island voted:

> In answer to the petition of Simon Mendes, David
> Brown, & associates being Jews, presenting to this As-
> sembly bearing date June 24, 1684, we declare that, they
> may expect as good protection here as any stranger
> being not of our nation residing amongst us, in his Maj-
> esty's Collony, ought to have, being obedient to his
> Majesty's laws.

Toward the end of the seventeenth century the
Newport community was much increased by a large
group of Jewish settlers who came from Curaçao.
These Jews, like their coreligionists already living
in the city, were of Spanish-Portuguese origin. Previous to their settlement in Curaçao, they had lived
in Holland, whither they had escaped either from
the Spanish or the Portuguese Inquisition. It was
their skill in commercial pursuits as well as their
diligence that induced the Dutch Government to
persuade them to aid in the settlement of Curaçao
in order to promote the commerce and welfare of
the island. With this natural energy and ability

which they immediately set to good use they brought
new grace and growth to Newport.

The growth of the Jewish community was characteristic of the growth of the city in general. The
Jews found the city of Newport in the very beginning of the century in its full bloom. Before the
century was half passed, the city doubled its population. In 1712, when John Mumford surveyed the
streets of Newport and noted "Jew's Street" on his
map, he remarked: "The town had grown to be the
admiration of all and was the metropolitan". When
Dean Berkeley, the famous English philosopher,
was greeted by people of all nationalities upon his
arrival in Newport in 1729, he is quoted as having
said: "The town of Newport is the most thriving
place in all America for bigness."

Indeed it was. And the "bigness" was not solely
in the economic and commercial pursuits of the
island but equally so, and perhaps more so, in religious, cultural and social enterprises. In view of
our knowledge of the religious toleration that existed in this colony since its inception, we are not
surprised at the words of Callender in 1739, that
"at this time" there were seven Churches in town,
besides the groups that had no regular places of
worship. It is a mark of the vitality of religion in
the life of the people at a time when they enjoyed
the abundance of plenty, to note in a town of but
twenty-five small streets and about a half dozen
lanes and wharfs, three Baptist, two Congrega-

tional, one Church of England, and one Friends house of worship.

Early in the eighteenth century, James Franklin, a brother of the famous Benjamin, established in Newport a printing press which produced a newspaper, published religious discourses and sermons and a good share of secular material. In 1730, Newport had a Philosophical Society in which a chronicler reports: "The Quaker, the Baptist, the firm supporter of the Church of England maintained each his part; but the Quaker preacher and the Jewish Rabbi, alike tenacious of their rules of doctrine, listened respectfully to the preaching of Berkeley." This was succeeded in 1747 by the Redwood Library, which rendered the whole mass of society much better informed in general literature and attracted "many men of science and erudition, who from time to time made Newport their abode."

Among the founders, members and contributors of the library were a proportionate number of Jews. In the portion of the original collection preserved today, there are a number of Hebrew texts, among them the philosophic book "Mateh Dan" by the Haham David Nieto, which was the gift of Naphtaly Hart Myers.

As the city prospered spiritually and culturally so it prospered commercially, in which members of the Jewish Community played an important part. As early as 1699, we hear of Isaac Cohen de Lara who had shipped goods from Rhode Island to New

York which were seized by a private vessel. Judah Hays and Moses Levy while still merchants in New York had business relationships with Jewish and non-Jewish merchants in Newport. It was Newport's commercial progress that attracted them to settle there. By the middle of the century Jewish merchants of Newport owned seven vessels used for colonial and foreign trade.

As active as were the Jews in business, just so active were they in manufacturing. As early as 1705, they had introduced the manufacture of soap into the colony. They joined in the establishment of foundries of brass and iron and conducted many other trades.

James Lucena, one of the refugees, as is attested by a resolution of the Assembly introduced the manufacture of Castille Soap in the colony. He had "acquired from the King's manufactory in Portugal the true method of making soap." And even a "Scotch Snuff Manufactory, between Lopez, Rivera, and Cardoza in Comy," was established.

The Jews were even represented in the medical profession at that early date. In 1761 Doctor Francis Lucena, also a refugee, a brother of James, practiced his profession in an office in the house of his brother.

By the middle of the century, Newport had attracted to its shores a number of wealthy Marrano families from Spain and Portugal who added greatly to the commercial prosperity of the city. The two most important were the Rivera and Lopez families.

In the seventeen-forties the Riveras established the first spermaceti candle factory. The manufacture of spermaceti candles within a short time was destined to surpass other industries in the colony.

It may not be amiss to recount here an incident associated with Jacob Rodriguez Rivera, the principal member of the family. Jacob was famous for his honesty. After a business failure when he had been declared bankrupt and his creditors satisfied, he again amassed considerable wealth. At a banquet he gave for all his former creditors, he astonished them by putting before each a draft for the exact amount, plus interest, that he had owed them.

The standing of the Lopez family may be gathered from the fact that in 1753, the General Assembly granted a license to Moses Lopez for the manufacture of potash, because of the advantages to Great Britain and the colonies and because "the said Moses, by assistance of a particular friend that is not in this country, has made himself master of the true art and mystery of making potash, which is known to very few in the kingdom." Apparently then as now a refugee could not disclose any name of "a particular friend that is not in this country" for fear that the friend might be apprehended in the land of persecution.

Moses Lopez was also granted certain exemptions by the General Assembly because of his Service as a translator of Spanish communications for the government.

Into this environment, where Jew and non-Jew

though worshipping separately in different forms and languages, but with the same aspirations, met on equality in the street, in the home, in the club or society, at the library, in the factory, on the vessel and in the store, came Aaron Lopez, a refugee from the Inquisition.

The date of Aaron's arrival in Newport has been given variously by different writers as between 1746 and 1754. The Naturalization papers of Aaron Lopez show that he settled in Newport on October 13, 1752.

No sufferings from the past are imprinted so deeply in the heart of the Jew as the persecution in Spain and Portugal and none have left such wounds in Israel as those inflicted in the Iberian Peninsula.

The Inquisition was introduced into the kingdom of Castile, Aragon, and Navarre by Ferdinand V and Isabella the Catholic. The victims were the thousands of Jewish families who accepted baptism during the cruel persecution of 1391 in order to save their lives, but who secretly in face of all dangers preserved their love for Judaism, Jewish law and custom.

Suspicion of Judaizing led to imprisonment and torture or to what at times was a more fortunate fate, execution by burning alive or in the case of a penitent after strangulation.

The prisons of the Inquisition with their torture chambers that can still be seen in some cities in Spain, had small, dark, damp and dirty underground little rooms with stone walls and iron bars. The prisoner's food was dry bread and water. In danger of such fate and imprisonment Aaron Lopez escaped his native city, Lisbon, Portugal.

It is said that a person's character, career and outlook in life is determined early in his life before he even advances much into the teens. If this is so then the character of Aaron Lopez was moulded by an environment clothed in fear and secrecy, suspicion and apprehension. He was born into a family of Marranos who for centuries through dread of the "Holy Office" of the Inquisition had led a dual life and personality. It may be of significance to note that only eight years before Aaron's birth a renowned physician, bearing the same "Christian" name as Aaron, Doctor Duarte Lopez, probably a member of the same family after whom Aaron was later named, was condemned by the Inquisition as an adherent to Judaism.

Aaron Lopez was born in Lisbon, in 1731. His father was Dom Diego Jose Lopez, a man "much respected and esteemed in Portugal." Aaron, one of three children born to Diego from his second marriage, was baptized according to the Catholic rite and christened Duarte. As far as one could observe Dom Diego was a strict observer of the rites of the Church and he gave his son Duarte as well as his other children, Jose, Michael, and Elizabeth from his first marriage, and Henry and Gabriel from his second marriage, a strict religious upbringing in accordance with the doctrine of the Church. If we are to judge by the beautiful hand-

writing and well written letters in Portuguese and
English which Aaron wrote in his later days as a
businessman in Newport, he must have received a
good training and education as a youth.

With all the rites of the Church, Duarte married
Anna, a close relative, also a Marrano. This was
the usual custom. The Marranos married mostly
within their own group. Anna bore Duarte a daughter who was christened Catherine.

Dom Diego Lopez and his family were Christians, however, only in appearance. As was customary among the Marranos, while they openly confessed Christianity and observed the rites and rituals
of the Church, they secretly observed and followed
the laws and rites of Judaism in whatever manner
possible. Within the family the father or mother
continued the tradition of teaching the children to
observe some parts of the Jewish ritual secretly,
thus keeping them united at least in part with the
religion of their fathers. As a consequence Jose, the
oldest son from the first marriage of Diego, having
been suspected of Judaizing by the Inquisition escaped the country while his father was still alive.
He was the first of the brothers to come through
England to America and to become known as Moses.
Another of Diego's sons escaped to Savannah la
Mar, Jamaica, where he adopted the name Abraham.

If one member of the family was suspected by the
Inquisition all the rest were spied upon and watched
carefully. Spies planted within the home followed
the steps of every member of the household and

reported back to the Holy Office. Duarte, too, must have been under close and scrupulous observation. And no doubt he was correctly suspected of Judaizing, for upon the earliest opportunity he, his wife and daughter made their way to the New World landing in Newport, where they found a haven of refuge from the persecution in Portugal. They were accompanied by Aaron's brother Gabriel who later was known as David. Henry, the third brother, had died in Lisbon as a young boy.

In the New World, Duarte and his family as well as his brother openly confessed Judaism by submitting to all necessary rites including circumcision, which in their native land was tantamount to suicide. Duarte and Anna were remarried with the traditional Jewish ceremony. His name was changed to Aaron. Hers to Abigail. Their daughter's name they changed to Sarah.

On October 30, 1752—in the earliest letter of the preserved Lopez correspondence—Daniel Gomez wrote from New York to Aaron, the newly arrived refugee and recently converted Marrano to Judaism, and expressed his delight that Aaron had finally reached Newport safely after a long and tedious voyage. In this letter Gomez congratulates Aaron on having "recibido el Sangre del Fermamento"—having received the blood of the covenant (circumcision)—and become faithful in the adherence to the "Holy Law", together with his wife, daughter and brother.

Dr. Ezra Stiles, a Congregational minister in

Newport and later president of Yale University, in
his diary under date March 27, 1775, recalls this
event when he records: "Attended the funeral of
Mr. David Lopez, who died yesterday morning aet.
61, and was this day at noon buried in the Jews
Burying Ground. He came from Portugal a few
years ago, and with his two sons was circumcised,
having been obliged to live secreted in Portugal."

So deep was the impression of the necessity of
secrecy in the observance of the Jewish religion that
out of habit, some of the Jewish women who came
here from Inquisition to Freedom, as they walked
the streets of Newport would tell their rosaries
while they repeated their Jewish prayers. This habit
had been acquired in Spain and Portugal for the
purpose of lending the appearance of Catholic form
should they be surprised at their devotions.

After Aaron's arrival in Newport, Abigail bore
him six more children. On May 14, Abigail died at
the youthful age of thirty-six. The children of this
marriage also died very young.

A year after Abigail died, Aaron remarried.
Readers of the Newport Mercury on August 29,
1763, found this notice: "Last Wednesday (August
24) was married Mr. Aaron Lopez, of this town,
Merchant, to Miss Sarah Rivera, daughter of Jacob
Rodriguez Rivera, Merchant." From this marriage
there were ten children, two of whom curiously
enough were named Jacob.

From a portrait of Aaron Lopez painted by the
famous Gilbert Stuart, of whom incidentally Aaron

Lopez was an early patron, the elegance of the man can be seen. One wonders little at the remark of the Hessian diarist who was astonished to note on his visit to Newport, in 1778, that the Jewish people do not differ in dress or in appearance from the rest of the population. Aaron in colonial apparel, from his cocked hat and white wig to his buckled shoes, his lace-trimmed shirt with its large collar and elaborate cravat, his neatly trimmed vest with silver buttons and his flowing cape, must have appeared not much different from a royal member of the British Court and must have been a very impressive gentleman. Only his piercing black eyes and olive-tinted skin betrayed his foreign origin and his birth on the Iberian Peninsula.

As soon as possible under the existing naturalization laws it was Aaron's desire to identify himself completely with his adopted country. Having had difficulty to be naturalized in Rhode Island because of some political reasons on the part of the members of the Superior Court and the General Assembly, Aaron became naturalized in Massachusetts, where he did considerable business and owned some property.

To satisfy all the requirements Lopez moved to Swansea, Massachusetts, just across the Rhode Island border, where he established his residence temporarily. He secured the necessary recommendation of good behavior and character from the colony of Rhode Island, which testified that:

Aaron Lopez professing the Jewish Religion Inhabitant
of the Colony in which he resided for the Space of Seven
Years last past without having been absent from the
same at any Time so long as Two Months. And that
he has ever deported himself as a good and loyal Subject
of His Britanic Majesty.

On October 15, 1762, Aaron was naturalized in
the Superior Court of Judicature of Taunton, as a
resident from Swansea and Newport. In the standard oath required, the words "upon the true faith
of a Christian" were crossed out.

Aaron came to Newport to his half brother
Moses, who preceded him there by a few years, and
who by the time Aaron came was well established in
the spermaceti industry. Moses was a recognized
merchant in Newport as early as 1746. It was he
who introduced in the colony the manufacture of
potash and translated the Spanish documents for
the Legislature. Very likely Aaron joined his
brother in some business enterprise and acquired
his experience of Rhode Island trade from him.

The early business career of Aaron Lopez can
only be surmised. That he was imbued with a genial
business spirit and that he possessed great ability
coupled with aptitude for mercantile pursuits can
be judged from his subsequent business enterprises.
However, having been by nature a person who did
things by scrupulous calculations, Aaron's beginnings
in trade and commerce were moderate and followed
the lines of all newcomers to the colony and the
newly arrived immigrants.

Three ideas were uppermost in his mind, which
with his natural capacity for business organization
and characteristically energetic nature led to his
success. The three ideas, which look simple, were
matters of great import. First, Lopez thought that
a good way to promote business and make it profitable and possible even without having much money
on hand was by the process of barter or exchange
of goods. Secondly, he was of the opinion that it
would be most advantageous and profitable to handle all kinds of merchandise. This was in essence the
idea of the Department Store. And finally, Lopez
came upon the idea that the most efficient way of
handling exports and imports is by having a business
factor or agent, to be exact, a field man, in the place
whereto merchandise is being sent to be sold, and
where other merchandise should be bought and sent
back to Newport. Thus the agent being in the place,
would ascertain the kind of merchandise needed in
that particular area, while at the same time he would
buy and prepare a cargo of goods to be ready for
reloading and for return. This would save time and
money, besides preventing blind guesses as to the
kind of merchandise to be exported and imported.

The commercial career of Aaron Lopez, thus follows a process of evolution based on these three
fundamental principles, which he followed very skil-
fully.

His first venture was the manufacture of spermaceti products, which had begun in Newport in the
seventeen-forties, by Jacob Rodriguez Rivera. The

importance to Lopez, however, seemed to have been the distribution of the spermaceti products rather than the manufacture. And in distribution, Lopez had his eye on commerce. Thus only two years after his arrival in Newport, we find him in correspondence with one Paul Tew of Providence to exchange with him spermaceti candles for tea and other products. Gradually he extended these barter enterprises to other colonies, confining himself to the coast and the nearest ports.

Spermaceti products involved whaling. Hence it was necessary for Mr. Lopez to contact and engage whalers. For this he engaged Henry Lloyd of Boston as the middleman between him and the whalers, while at the same time, Lloyd also acted as his business agent or factor in Boston, helping to distribute the manufactured Newport products in Boston for the exchange of imported and other goods.

For about ten years Lopez confined himself to the manufacture of spermaceti products, carrying on at the same time a coastwise shipping business, extending to Boston, New York, Philadelphia and Charleston.

Aaron Lopez had a conservative nature. Before entering on a business venture, he made careful preparations, though he was willing to undertake enterprises involving risks and great financial investments. He made mistakes in business calculations; but seldom did he repeat an error.

The Seven Years' War which began in Europe in 1756 between England and Prussia against France and Austria, was preceded by two years of fighting in America, where it was known as the French and Indian War. The conditions of the war, as well as the various Navigation Acts of the British Government, made shipping business uncertain and risky. It was the cause of many business failures and of general financial depression. During this time, Aaron concentrated on the manufacture and wholesale distribution of spermaceti candles in which he prospered. And so, only nine years after his arrival, on November 5, 1761, when the Newport manufacturers entered into a "Spermaceti Candle Agreement," Aaron Lopez & Co. was among the signatories. This combination controlling the spermaceti trade has been compared to later organizations such as Shell and Standard Oil.

Though Lopez prospered in his manufacture of spermacti products, he nevertheless desired to expand his commercial activity beyond the coastal engagements, and trade direct with foreign ports.

His desire was to expand and to engage in oversea export and import trade, which though it involved greater risks, promised much greater returns. As would be expected he had his eye on British trade, which was the popular thing at the time. His first contacts were attempted rather early in his career through his correspondents in Great Britain, William Stead of London and Henry Cruger, Jr. of Bristol. Already early in the sixties of the century Lopez corresponded with them, and before long his ships Charlotte, America, Friendship, Newport

Packet, were on their way to English ports, with cargoes consigned to Henry Cruger, Jr., who became his business representative there. Lopez preferred his exports and imports to go through Bristol, where merchandise could be disposed of easily, and on the other hand where English merchandise could be obtained more reasonably than elsewhere. His plan was to send vessels to Bristol with log-wood, mahogany, building lumber, oil and other spermaceti products, while obtaining there for import to Newport, English drygoods, hardware and other English products, for which there was a good market in New England and elsewhere in the colonies.

For a time Lopez must have been the only Newport trader with Bristol, as seems to be indicated from one of his letters to Cruger, in which in 1765, he writes: "From the advantage of being the only Trader that undertakes Steady Commerce with Bristol that I made my address to your House worthy some Notice."

For this trade with Bristol, Lopez needed better ships and brigantines to be able to stand the long voyages on the ocean. Accordingly he began to construct new brigantines, sloops and schooners or to reinforce or add new decks to his old boats.

In this enterprise he also used the art of barter. Typical of this are some of the agreements between Aaron Lopez and some ship builders. On one occasion Cromwell & Caleb Childs agree to build for Aaron Lopez a new upper deck on a sloop called Industry in exchange for English goods. John Kelly

agrees to deliver a boat of about a hundred and fifteen tons to Aaron Lopez to be paid for in English
goods, tea, sugar and New England rum. Benjamin
Bowers of Swansea agrees to build a sloop for
Aaron Lopez sixty-two feet long to be paid for in
part in molasses, West India goods, flour, pork,
European drygoods and a little cash. Nathan Miller
agrees to build brigs and schooners and add new
decks to old ships in consideration for the merchandise and price that Sylvester Child of Warren received for building his boats for the Newport
merchant, namely English goods, hardware and
crockery ware.

The following is a typical agreement:

It is hereby agreed between the Subscribers that John O.
Kelly of Warren of the One Part & Aaron Lopez of
Newport on the Other Part, That said Kelly shall deliver on float soon as possibly he can a certain Brig. now
almost finished Burthen About One Hundred and Fifteen Tons which he is to Compleat & finish in a Work-
manlike manner, to the approbation of any indifferent
Ship Carpenter, for which Vessell, when so finished he is
to receive at the Rate of Eleven Dollars per Ton Payable
in Englishe Goods Excepting Sixty weight of good Tea
at three Shillings & Nine Pence Levy and One Hogshead
Sugar of an inferior quality at Twenty two Shillings &
Six Pence & Ct. Three Barrells dt°. of a good Quality at
forty eight Shillings & One Hd. New Engl⁴. Rum at
One Shilling & tenpence Pr Gallo.,

NewPort Aprill 6,th 1772

In the early sixties of the century Lopez and his
father-in-law Rivera joined in the shipping business.

Together with Rivera, Lopez made several additional attempts at shipping ventures to European
ports. He also apparently attempted to send some
ships to African coasts. But none of the ventures
proved successful to be continued on chance without
scrupulous thought about them. In fact some proved
a total failure and plunged Aaron into debt for over
fifteen thousand pound sterling owed to William
Stead in London and Henry Cruger, Jr. in Bristol.

Aaron Lopez did not become discouraged by the
European failure of his early ventures. Resolute to
pay back his debts which were constantly on his
mind and to continue his commercial activity, Aaron
turned to the West India trade, which was more
promising, putting into it his heart and soul and all
the talent and resources at his command. Lopez
refers to this change of business orientation in the
following words in a letter to Cruger in 1767:

> By dear bought experience I have learnt that the method
> of making remittance from these parts thro' the Guinea
> Channell, as also that of sending New Ships to the Eng-
> lish market, have proved very disheartnening of Late
> Years. Therefore, I have timely alter'd the course of my
> Business and adopted the old tract of remitting by way
> of West Indies, a trade where my Spermaceti, and Oil
> Connexions will afford many peculiar advantages not
> common to other people and having this year launched
> largely into it, have reason to expect (Deo volente) that
> I shall have it in my power to make you next Summer
> and Fall some Considerable returns on the arrival of my
> Jamaica men.

Aaron Lopez had good contacts with the West

Indies. His half brother Abraham lived in Savannah la Mar, Jamaica. Early in 1767, Aaron's daughter Sally married Abraham Pereira Mendes who
hailed from Kingston, Jamaica, where his family
was residing.

A glimpse into the nature of this romance gathered from the Lopez correspondence is very interesting. Isaac Pereira Mendes, a brother of Abraham writes to Aaron Lopez on February 15, 1767:

> The choice of my Brother Abraham to your daughter
> Sally, for his Consort has merited much our Approba-
> tion, as also that of my honourd Mother. The ameable-
> ness of your daughter, the Bright Corrector and honour
> of yours and familys, as much in these parts, as those of
> ancient, in Portugal, cannot butt give us in generall the
> greatest satisfaction; that my Brother has united himself
> with; which is doing honour to the Memory of our
> Worthy and Honoured Father.

For a short period Abraham Lopez acted as
Aaron's representative in Jamaica. The untimely
death of his wife and other circumstances forced
Abraham to decline the post, in whose place Aaron
sent his son-in-law Abraham Pereira Mendes as his
factor in the West Indies.

Mendes, unfortunately, had neither the ability
nor the responsibility to handle the affairs of his
father-in-law. Though he did not neglect to add in
the postscripts of many a letter he sent to Lopez,
his love for his wife, Sally, and especially "I beg
you'll not neglect giving my little Jacob many Kisses

at the Recet of this...or to my Litte Jacob whom
you'll embrace with 100 kisses for me," Mendes
was a disappointment to his father-in-law. To handle his business affairs properly and in accordance
with his wishes, Lopez engaged as his West India
factor Captain Benjamin Wright, known as "the
Presbyterian Old Yankee", who was one of the
shrewdest traders in the Carribbean. Captain
Wright served Lopez in a threefold capacity. He
sailed the vessels as a Captain, acted as sales-agent
or factor, and was also a partner. The efficiency of
Captain Wright prospered a great deal Lopez's
trade. Wright would stay a little while in the West
Indies to find a market for the goods consigned to
him, in the meanwhile buying up products from the
planters which he prepared for return shipment,
and which he would manage to be first to send out
and reach Lopez in Newport before the vessels of
anyone else.

The West India trade proved very profitable to
Aaron. In the majority of cases he used his own
vessels. By 1769, writes one historian:

> The clouds began to break; golden days were soon to
> shine on the house of Lopez. A rare combination of
> business talent was now at work in Newport and Ja-
> maica: Aaron Lopez was as ardent and imaginative a
> merchant as could be found in North America. Like all
> successful traders he had made mistakes—the Bristol
> episode was one—but he had a good memory and an
> ingenious mind. Seldom did he repeat an error, and he
> was always ready to try an experiment. This was the
> kind of man who brought the golden age to Newport.

Within a short while he paid his debts built up a considerable fortune and became a principal merchant in Newport, referred to as a "Merchant Prince." He did not neglect, nevertheless, the coastwise and European trade which by this time also improved and brought him handsome profits.

The success of Lopez's West India business ventures did not stop his business dealings locally in Newport. There Lopez continued his wholesale and retail trade in his store and warehouse on Lopez Wharf, where he employed many people. One of his employees was Enoch Lyon who, for "Victuals, Lodging, and all contingent Needfull charges, Excepting Clothing" and fifty Spanish Mill dollars yearly, agreed to work for Lopez for a period of four years "ready to obey his Lawfull Commands, relating only to Traffick, Merchandising and Bookkeeping." Together with his employees worked also Aaron's children, in whatever capacity eligible.

Aaron extended his business enterprises even to that of builder. In this case too he used the method of barter. On February 26, 1772, Aaron Lopez contracted to build a "good substantial house" thirty-six feet front, two stories high, with a finished cellar and all improvements, for eight hundred and nine Spanish Silver dollars, which he had built for himself only eight days before, by Charles Spooner, and for which he paid in spermaceti candles and English goods.

At the same time he continued his active interest in the fishing and whaling industry. A typical example of his activity in this field is the following:

Newport Rhode Island April 22.^{d} 1771

It is hereby agreed between Aaron Lopez of Newport Merchant of the One part and Thomas Earnshey & Company Fishermen now bound on a Voyage to Gaspee there to be employed in the Codfishing of the other Part

That said Lopez shall furnish said Earnshey & Company with Provisions Salt, One fishing Boat, Fishing Tackle and all Utensils necessary for said voyage and shall have the same together with said Earnshey and Company transported to Gaspee aforesaid without any Expense to them the said Fishermen.

That said Earnshey & Company shall furnish and carry with them to Gaspee aforesaid Two fishing Boats of their own property to be there employed in common with the other Boat in said Fishing Business on account of the Parties without any Expense to sd. Company for carrying said Boats to Gaspee.

That said Lopez shall send a vessell to Gaspee aforesaid where he will endeavor she shall by the Twenty-fifth Day of August next and there tarry till said Fishermen shall have compleated their Business when she shall receive aboard said Company of Fishermen together with their Craft and all the fish Oil & Gurry they may have taken and made and bring the same to this port without any charge to them the sd. Fishermen

That at their Arrival here all the Fish, Oil & Gurry that shall be taken & made by them the said Fishermen during said Voyage shall be fairly divided between said Lopez and said Company of Fishermen in the following Proportions vis Said Lopez shall receive Seven Sixteenths of the Fish and one half of the Oil & Gurry and said Earnshey & Company shall receive Nine Sixteenths

of the Fish and One half of the Oil & Gurry without
any other Charge or Expense for any of the afore mentioned Articles or Services to either of the Parties than
is above expressed.

Lopez's commercial activities can partially be
gauged from the record of the year 1768. In that
year Lopez sailed five vessels to the West Indies,
four to Europe, one to Africa and thirty-seven down
the coast. As the years went on, up till about 1775
his shipping and all business ventures and with it his
wealth increased.

The extensive commercial activities of Aaron
Lopez brought to Newport its "Golden Era" before
the American Revolution. That Newport was the
commercial rival of New York and other American
ports is attested by the statement: "He was thought
a bold prophet who said then that New York might
one day equal Newport." From five to six hundred
vessels traded from the port of Newport. It may
sound curious today, but from this time we have a
letter addressed to "New York near Newport,
Rhode Island." Aaron Lopez is said to have been
the largest shipowner and merchant in Newport at
this period, having acquired entire or part ownership to over a hundred vessels. Records now extant
show Lopez's ownership of thirty-nine of these.

Mr. Lopez's residence was at 131-133 Thames
Street, the buildings extending to the water. The
warehouse towards the pier on Newport harbor
was a large three story building. The first floor
was used for a storehouse. The second was used

for the Lopez offices. The third floor, which extended in length over two hundred feet was used as a sail loft. The wharf is still named "Lopez Wharf". The wide reputation of Aaron Lopez invited many to advertise their businesses as being located "opposite Mr. Lopez's" or "next to Mr. Lopez's."

In the vaults of the Newport Historical Society there are deposited some of the Lopez business books and manuscript correspondence. Among them are no less than twenty-one Letter Books, containing correspondence from 1752 until 1782; twenty Day Books; two Letter Copy Books; three folders and a box of miscellaneous papers, such as agreements, contracts, drafts, notes and personal correspondence; and several ledgers, invoice books, shipping and receipt books. Much of the correspondence now preserved is in mercantile Spanish of the period.

The vast amount of manuscript material in the Newport Historical Society, which constitutes only part of the Lopez business records, for a great many more exist in other archives, gives an indication of the magnitude and extent of Lopez's commercial activities. This can also be gauged from the fact that among the four hundred and forty-five letters, sailing orders, invoices, bills of lading and trading agreements pertaining to Rhode Island Commerce between 1726 and 1774, published by the Massachusetts Historical Society, two hundred and twenty-five relate directly to Aaron Lopez.

Upon examination of the records we find that

vessels of Lopez left for Newfoundland, Surinam, West Indies, Madeira, Lisbon, Gibraltar, Cape Nicholas, Cape Francois, Amsterdam, Bristol, and Curaçao, besides to all the shores of the American colonies.

The names of some of the vessels are interesting: Ship Jacob, Sloop Abigail, Brig Hannah, and other names like, Active, Friendship, Providence, Cupid, Ann, Peace & Plenty, Sally, Venus, Hope and Humbird. Some of the Brigs weighed one hundred and fifteen tons, and had two decks. Of the ships hired to carry cargo for Lopez, he would usually assure the captain with the payment for the entire boat or the largest part of its value if seized. An instance of this we find in the agreement between John Strange of Freetown, Massachusetts, a mariner and owner of the sloop King-Fisher and Aaron Lopez, in which the former agrees to "freight let unto Aaron Lopez the said Sloop, together with the Rigging, Sails, and all other Appurtenances necessary for the Performance of a Voyage to be made hence to Cape Nichola Mole on Hispaniola, and from thence back to Newport" on the sole risk of Strange except in the case of seizure. And "in case of Seizure of said Sloop, the said Lopez to pay said Strange the Sum of Two Hundred Pounds Sterling." Such agreements were also made in case the boat would be lost, as is instanced in the agreement between Aaron Lopez with Eleazar Trevet, where the latter agrees to let Lopez the sloop called "The Dolphin," measuring seventy-three ton and valued at three hundred and ninety pounds, and of which Lopez agrees to pay half if the sloop is lost in the voyage.

Every conceivable kind of merchandise, from needles to riding carriages was handled through the ports of Newport. It is obvious that much of the exports from Newport to other ports had been brought there from foreign ports. The ships that sailed to Europe, South America and the West Indies, brought back a variety of merchandise which was sold either in the home colony or else in the other English colonies in North America. Newport served as the export and import clearing house with Aaron Lopez as the executive.

In his commercial success Lopez did not forget God and the Religion of his fathers. Having professed Judaism openly, Aaron joined the Congregation Yeshuat Israel, which had been in existence in Newport, according to tradition, well nigh a century. When he came from Lisbon and openly professed his faith, he identified himself completely with the Jewish community.

Since the founding of the Congregation Yeshuat Israel the Congregation worshiped in private homes or in rented rooms, not having a regular place of worship. Whether the small house near the cemetery served as a mortuary chapel or a small synagogue for occasional services can not be told. The first thing contemplated by the Marranos who arrived in Newport in the middle of the eighteenth century

INTERIOR OF TOURO SYNAGOGUE, NEWPORT,
R. I.

was the erection of a sanctuary dedicated to the God of Israel, a synagogue where they might freely chant the psalmodies, commune with God of their fathers and practice the rites of which in the lands of their birth they had been deprived.

Aaron Lopez threw himself heart and soul into the movement to build the synagogue.

The first mention of Aaron Lopez in association with the Congregation Yeshuat Israel is in connection with the building of the synagogue. On March 1, 1759, when the Congregation sent a letter of appeal to the Congregation Shearith Israel of New York, asking assistance in the erection of a synagogue, Aaron Lopez was one of the signers.

On August 1, 1759, the cornerstones of what is now the oldest synagogue in America were laid on a plot of land then on Griffin Street and now known as Touro Street, which cost—in present exchange—$187.50. Aaron Lopez, the one time Marrano living as a Catholic, had the distinction of laying the first cornerstone as the lay leader of the Jewish community and an outstanding citizen of the community.

Peter Harrison, who apparently had no professional training as an architect, but was a "cultivated amateur", who had to his credit the architectural designs of many outstanding structures, was engaged as the architect. He rendered his services entirely gratuitously. Harrison combined in the plan of the Newport synagogue his particular artistic architectural style with the traditional Synagogue architecture of the Spanish-Portuguese Jews. The combination invites admiration.

The color scheme and design of the preserved painting of the Ten Commandments on the top of the Ark suggests that it was painted by the famous Gilbert Stuart, no doubt as a gesture of reciprocity to Aaron Lopez one of his early patrons.

The building, begun with the laying of the corner-stones, continued at a slow pace. The days of "rush" were still in the future. It was not easy to get building material. The bricks had to be imported from abroad. The 196,715 bricks that were to be used for the structure were paid for on August 25, 1760.

After practically four years of building, the dedication of the new synagogue took place on December 2, 1763. The ceremony of the dedication was calculated to bring out all the beauties of the Synagogue and its service. The invited audience consisted of Jews and non-Jews, including a great number of notables of the city and guests from other localities. Early in the afternoon the people began to gather in the synagogue, the men taking their places downstairs, the women seating themselves in the balcony. The consecration service made a deep impression on all present.

The synagogue which has not been changed since, either in the interior or in the exterior, measures but about forty by thirty-five feet and stays at an acute angle with the street so that the Ark where the Scrolls are found is in the exact east. The plan of the interior is a miniature parallel to the ancient Holy Temple in Jerusalem.

From the domed ceiling are suspended five large brass candelabra, one of which, according to tradition, once adorned a monastery in Spain during the Inquisition. In front of the Ark, also suspended from the ceiling, hangs the perpetual lamp which burns continuously. The Reading Desk from where the prayers are chanted in Hebrew in the old traditional melodies is in the centre of the synagogue.

The balcony which is reserved for the women worshippers and which is ascended from the side room adjacent to the synagogue at the outer northern wall is supported by twelve columns extending to the ceiling. These columns are said to represent the twelve tribes of Israel. The entire structure has the richness of simplicity and the glory of sanctity. It is a miniature of the Temple in Jerusalem, where

> The weary ones, the sad, the suffering
> All found their comfort in the Holy Place
> And children's gladness and men's gratitude
> Took voice and mingled in the chant of praise.

On the eve of the Revolution the city boasted a population of eleven thousand among whom were eleven hundred of the Jewish religion with Aaron Lopez as the lay leader.

Aaron Lopez was a staunch supporter of the synagogue. Of the five candelabra to this day preserved in the house of worship one bears the inscription:

"The Gift of Aaron Lopez Anno Mundi 5530."
Among the scrolls in the Ark, which a contemporary
observed, there was a "Holy Scroll with Silver
bells of Great value," the gift of Aaron Lopez.
When Doctor Stiles visited the synagogue on the
"Sabbath of Passover," and heard the various offerings made by some of the members, he observed:
"Large offerings or Alms were made to probably
Fourty dollars as one of the Jews estimated and I
believe true; for sundry offered Chai Livre i.e. £16
or two dollars and I judge Mr. Aaron Lopez offered
ten or a dozen of these Chai."

The extent of his benefactions may be judged
from the fact that his earnest efforts and generous
gifts were remembered every Yom Kippur Eve when
the minister of the synagogue offered a special
prayer for him.

In fact during the time the synagogue was closed,
Aaron Lopez was considered the founder of it. By
the will of Abraham Touro, the son of the first minister of the synagogue, a sum of money was left for
the synagogue and for the city to keep the street
upon which the synagogue was situated in perpetual
repair. Moses Lopez of Newport, at that time in
New York, was asked to become a trustee of the
legacy left by Abraham Touro. Moses, refusing the
honor on the grounds of being in ill health, suggested in a letter to Stephen Gould of Newport, a
Christian in charge of the synagogue and cemetery,
taking care of the properties without any remun-
eration: "My deceased uncle Aaron Lopez was

founder of the Newport Synagogue and as he has
two sons yet alive, Joshua and Samuel Lopez, as
well as a grandson married in this city by the name
of Aaron L. Gomez, a man I can recommend to be
of greatest integrity, I think they have the prior
right to be appointed with two more men of the
Congregation in this place."

During the time Aaron Lopez was in Leicester,
Massachusetts, where he went at the occupation of
Newport by the British, the Congregational Church
of Newport, which had been made unfit for services
desired the use of the synagogue. Mr. Channing,
the minister, on behalf of his congregation applied
to Moses Seixas on several occasions for permis-
sion to use the synagogue. Mr. Seixas, who at this
time was the custodian of the building, addressed a
letter to Aaron Lopez on October 5th, 1780, writing: "Mr. Channing again applied for the use of
the Synagogue. I availed myself of the impropriety
of letting him have it, whilst I had not your sense
on the occasion and which had been requested by
his and Mr. Merchants desire."

As Aaron Lopez linked up the four corners of
the world by his commercial activities, so was he
a mediator between the Jewish groups in all these
parts of the world where his vessels landed. We
may recall here that in his day the Inquisition was
still active in Spain and Portugal. In a letter written by James Lucena to Aaron Lopez on January
19, 1771 from Savannah, Georgia, whereto apparently Lucena moved from Newport, he states: "I

have news by letters from Lisbon of our acquaintances in general . . . A inquiciçao decae mas nao se extinge . . . the Inquisition declines but is not extinguished." To help the refugees of the Inquisition, Lopez was instrumental in bringing over from Portugal to Newport upward to forty families. Evidence of his work on behalf of the refugees from the Inquisition exists in one of the letters dated November 18, 1766, addressed to Jeremiah Osborne, of the ship "Pitt" then about to sail from London to Lisbon, with a cargo of sea-coal: "Should any of my friends in Lisbon incline to come with you, I need not recommend you to use them with the same tenderness that I might expect myself from you, being well assured of your civil and obliging disposition."

Lopez was in constant receipt of letters from people abroad to send money and support them as he had been doing continuously. Whenever an itinerary representative of some charitable institution visited Newport for the purpose of soliciting funds or when appeals for funds were solicited by mail, Lopez would not only be the largest contributor, but would be instrumental in collecting much money from others. Invariably the visitors would be the guests of Mr. Lopez. On more than one occasion we find an entry in Stiles' diary: "This Afternoon the Rabbi came to visit me in Company with Mr. Lopez."

From the year 1770, we have a very interesting letter written in Hebrew interspersed in several places with Yiddish by a certain Abraham ha-Levi from Lisa, Poland, the native city of Haym Salomon the famous contributor to the success of the American Revolution, who visited Newport soliciting financial assistance.

Concerning this Abraham ha-Levi there is an entry in Stiles' Diary:

"The Jew visited me again to-day. His name is Abraham Levi aet. 44. I shewed him the Computa made by a German Rabbi placing the Appear[a]. . of the Messiah in 1783. He smiled, & said they looked for him every day. . . I accidentally sneezed & he prayed instantly. At sunset he excused himself & rose up & went to my East window & prayed by himself. & then returned & sat down again to discourse. He seems to be a man of Sobriety, spake of the Deity with uplifted hands & Eyes & with the most profound Reverence."

In the letter mentioned above ha-Levi thanks Mr. Lopez for the recommendation which he received from him which made it possible for him to obtain assistance in New York. The letter is unique. It reads in part:

Blessed be God.

Today the fourth day of the week, the New Moon of Iyar of the year 530 minor notations at New York.

From afar I send greetings of peace to the beloved the honorable sir, the exalted leader, dear and upright— May the splendor of his glorious name be praised among the wise—his excellency Aaron Lopez.—May his light be bright and shine forth as a brilliant lustre—and to his consort the praiseworthy and noble lady the wife of a scholar, the modest and pious—May she live long—and to his sons and his daughters—May they live long each and everyone of them.

I am informing you that I arrived here thanks be to God, in peace, and have delivered his letter in the correct manner, on account of it I have been well received. May God reward him doubly in the world to come. And for my part I say to my noble master—May his light be bright—thanks for the favors that I have received from him.

And there is nothing more to be said except, life and peace from the Lord of the Universe and from me his good friend, who remembers him for good at all times.

Such are the words of Abraham ha-Levi of Lissa—May that city be rebuilt and restored speedily in our day, Amen.

In the postscripts which exceed in length the body of the letter Abraham ha-Levi asks to be remembered to Rabbi Touro, to Mr. Jacob R. Rivera, to Hayim Levy, and his family, and to Aaron's brother and his family, wishing them peace, happiness and long life.

In religious life, Lopez, the former Marrano, was a strict observer of Jewish laws and traditions. He kept his place of business closed on Saturday, the Jewish Sabbath, and out of regard to the sentiments of the people among whom he lived he kept his stores closed from Friday sunset to Monday morning. Upon examination of his shipping books we find that none of his vessels left the port of Newport on a Saturday.

A diarist writing about Aaron Lopez and his

fellow Jews who settled in Leicester during the British occupation of Newport says:

> They always observed the rites and ceremonies of their law and their stores were closed from Friday until Monday morning. They were prudent, industrious and enterprising and many of them were elegant in their address and deportment and possessed an extensive knowledge of the world. They were always respected and esteemed by the inhabitants of the town and always seemed to remember with pleasure the kindness and civility they on their part received while residents there and availed themselves ever afterwards of every opportunity that presented to express these feelings, as many who experienced their attentions when in Newport would attest.

Mr. Lopez and his family were faithful observers of the Jewish dietary laws. While the Lopez family was in Leicester, David Lopez, Jr., who moved to Providence during the British occupation of Newport, reminds Aaron Lopez that: "Mr. Mendes promised to forward Goods from Tafts Tavern for Old Mr. Trevett which with the Wine and a bbl. of Casher Beef he engaged to send us may probably make a load sufficient to induce a Teamster to come down".

On July 9, 1781, Moses Seixas informs Aaron Lopez among other things: "My dear Mrs. Lopez may depend on having a reinforcement of Casher fat as soon as possible."

It is noteworthy that among the products sent from Newport by Lopez to the West Indies and other ports were "Jew Beef," to Barbados; "Casher Fatt," "Casher Tongues," and "Casher Cheeses" to Surinam and Jamaica. When the products left Newport, they were certified as "Casher" by the proper Jewish authorities in the town, and the certification was done within the walls of the Synagogue.

The certificates were signed by the Minister of the Congregation, or the Shohet. In a letter to Isaac Pereira Mendes in Withywood, Jamaica, under date February 13, 1767, Aaron Lopez writes:

> I have the pleasure to direct per Capt. James Potter bound for St. Anns in a brig of mine. He will forward you the same with the few small articles as per inclosed Invo. which I have taken the Liberty to trouble you with by way of Tryall; should it happen the Meat etc. is approved of & sells to any advantage I can supply larger Quantities. Annexed You'll find our Hazan's certificate of their being duly put up."

The life of the people at that time was permeated with the thought and spirit of God. This extended even to commercial enterprises. As an example of this we may quote one of the shipping forms of Aaron Lopez, dated December 17, 1771:

> Shipped by the Grace of GOD, in good Order and well conditioned, by Aaron Lopez on his Account & Risque in and upon the good Sloop called Sally whereof is Master, under God, for the present Voyage, John Nagus Junr., and now riding at Anchor in the Harbour of Newport and by GOD's Grace bound for Surinam— To say, Sixty Nine Quarter barrels, Eight half ditto & one Tun contg. Jew beef & Tongues, & Twenty One-Gallon Kegs Jew fatt....And so GOD send the good Sloop to her desired Port in Safety, Amen.

In the general life of the city, Aaron Lopez occupied a prominent place. He was a member of and contributor to the Redwood Library. He participated in every civic affair and was a guest of many public and communal functions.

The esteem with which Aaron Lopez was widely regarded for his enterprise and judgment is evidenced from the following. In August 1773, the General Assembly of Rhode Island in considering the matter of a petition of a number of merchants for the advancement of the valuable codfisheries "in and near the Gulf of St. Lawrence," and that "they may by Royal indulgence be permitted to prosecute their fishing business in its full extent at Isle Bonavanture, Isle Pierre, Point St. Peter and elsewhere in the Gulf of St. Lawrence, without obstruction or hinderance and that the fishing in those parts may by no means be converted into private property or monopolized by a company" passed the following vote:

> It is voted and resolved that Messrs. Aaron Lopez, George Gibbs, and William Vernon be, and they or the major part of them are hereby appointed a committee to prepare a draught of a letter respecting the matter set forth in the said petition to be sent to his Majesty's Secretary of State, and that they lay the same before the Assembly.

Messrs. Gibbs and Vernon were the foremost citizens and merchants of Newport. Yet, Lopez was named first and so was the chairman of the committee.

When Chief Judge Haymanden was visiting Newport in 1773, as a member of the British Court of
Royal Commissioners, he and his wife dined in Lopez's home. On this occasion Mr. and Mrs. Lopez
entertained a number of the leading citizens of Newport and their wives. The formal invitation on this
occasion has been preserved.

> Mr. and Mrs. Lopez present their best Respects to Mr.
> and Mrs. Dudley, and will be extremely happy in having
> their good Company's to join those of his Hon. Chief
> Judge Haymanden and Lady, who intends dining with
> Mr. Lopez to-day.

Aaron's friendship to all was indeed great. This
is attested by many contemporary observers. Wash-
burn in speaking of Lopez refers to him as "a man
universally esteemed and respected by a wide circle of personal friends." The same author states:

> His, Mr. Lopez's, style of living was generous and hos-
> pitable; and the furniture of his house, the plate upon
> his table, and the retinue of his servants, wore an air of
> magnificence among his less endowed neighbors; but
> the cordiality of his manners and his liberal hospitality
> disarmed all cavil and envy on their part.

In the same vein, the author continues his appraisal of Lopez together with the other Jewish
families that lived with him:

> Though differing from their neighbors on matters of
> religious faith, they won the confidence and esteem of all
> by their upright and honorable dealing, the kindliness and
> courtesy of their intercourse, and the liberality and pub-
> lic spirit which they evinced as citizens.

Early in the seventies of the eighteenth century Newport commerce began to decline. British disciplinary measures as expressed in the various Navigation and Tax Acts worked hardships on the shipping business. Aaron Lopez was among those who felt it most. Joining in the Non-importation Agreements with the rest of the merchants reduced much of his commercial activity. This did not discourage him or retire him from business. There was no way of foreseeing or preparing for the business calamities which were to accompany the outbreak of hostilities between Great Britain and the colonies. Many, of course, were optimistic enough to believe that hostilities would never break out, and that somehow the differences between the colonies and the mother country would be reconciled.

Lopez, apparently, was among them, as may be inferred from his agreement with John Strange, the owner of a sloop "King-Fisher," who agreed to carry goods for Lopez to Cape Nichola Mole on Hispaniola on March 4, 1774, with the stipulation: "in Case of Seizure of said Sloop, the said Lopez to Pay said Strange the Sum of Two Hundred Pounds Sterling." Lopez having been of a conservative nature and not inclined much to speculating, we must ascribe such and other risks taken by him to his optimism and faith in a peaceful settlement between Britain and the colonies. For when the outbreak did come Aaron like many of the others was unprepared for it, nor was he in a position to control matters to his benefit.

Many of his ships were at sea. Aaron did not see fit to liquidate his holdings in the West Indies. Perhaps he thought of preserving them by holding on to them, as values in the colonies began to crumble with the first shot. The consequences were, that when the first shot of the Revolution was fired it marked the ruin of the prosperous Aaron Lopez. His ships were seized and his goods confiscated by both sides in the conflict.

Yet Aaron Lopez espoused the cause of the Colonists and contributed to the cause of the Revolution whatever was in his ability.

In a memorial addressed to the Continental Congress by James Wilson and Wm. Lewis, we have a summary of Lopez's role in the conflict.

That Gentleman before the Commencement of the present War had Property to a very large Amount in the Island of Jamaica...In his attempts which Mr. Lopez has made to draw his Effects from Jamaica, his vessels have been captured by private armed Vessels...In order to avoid Similar Inconveniences in the future, he has desired and empowered us to apply to the Honorable Body in his Behalf, for Protection for his Property.

The Character of Mr. Lopez, as a Friend to the Liberties and Independence of the United States, is clear and unimpeached, as will be testified by some honorable Members of this House.

In 1776, the General Assembly of Rhode Island allowed Aaron the sum of £22 for gunpowder and a whale boat which had been taken over by the colony.

As the conflict continued living conditions in New-port began to be unbearable. The British had their eye on the seaport of Newport. Their plan was to cut it off from the rest of the colonies thereby dis-uniting them and depriving them of a port and a base.

On the approach of the British, Aaron Lopez together with his father-in-law Jacob Rodrigues Rivera, his son-in-law Abraham Pereira Mendes and their families as well as the Jacobs family— all told about seventy souls—left Newport for Leicester, Massachusetts, stopping for a short period in Providence.

Lopez refers to his settlement in Leicester in a letter to a friend in Philadelphia:

Since we left our place my Family, secure from sudden Alarms and the Cruel Ravages of an enraged Enemy; Such a one I have hitherto found in the small inland Township of Leicester in the Massachusetts Bay, where I pitched my Tent, erecting a proportionable one to the extent of my numerous Family on the Summit of a high healthy Hill, where we have experienced the civilities and hospitality of a kind Neighborhood; and moved in the same Sphere of Business I have been used to follow which altho much more contracted, it has fully answered my wishes.

In Leicester, Lopez purchased an estate and erected on it what was for that day "a large and elegant mansion" designed for a store and dwelling-house. While he was not able to pursue his busi-ness enterprises on as large a scale as in Newport his "Department Store" idea still prevailed and

served him in good stead. As much as possible he
continued his shipping business as well as his wholesale distribution of merchandise. Even from this
period there is a wealth of business records and correspondence, showing commercial negotiations involving shipping. But at this time it was mostly
coastwise and intercolonial.

The war of the Revolution was still raging.
Wherever battles were actually fought conditions
were frightful. The civilian population suffered no
less than the armed forces. The people in general
were in great plight. The outcome of the conflict
was uncertain. Families were moving from place to
place. All this was destructive to prosperous business enterprises.

Though successful in reopening some business
channels which were closed during the war, and
aided by his son Joseph and other members of his
family to continue his General Store in Leicester,
Aaron's business and wealth was on a constant decline. This decline can be gauged from his tax ac-
counts. During the year 1779, Aaron Lopez paid
£343. 15s. State tax for "Personal and Faculty"
property, and £91. 13s. 4d. "Town and County"
tax. In 1780, his tax bill for the State for "Personal
and Faculty" property amounted to £79. 25s. 10d.
and the Town and County tax bill for Real Estate
and Personal Estate and Faculty was £66. 21s. 1d.
altogether half of the previous year assessment.

In 1780, Congress granted Aaron a safe-conduct

whereby he succeeded in transferring some of his property from Jamaica to Leicester. He also won some lawsuits he had brought in the Court of Admiralty and Appeals for the return of his ships that had been taken as prizes by American privateers. But it all did not improve his financial condition.

In addition to the decline in business enterprises and in earnings from commercial transactions the value of money decreased immensely due to inflation of the currency which still more decreased Lopez's wealth.

After the departure of the British from Newport the city gradually regained commerce and shipping; but it missed the enterprising merchants from before the Revolution. It was not destined that Newport should again compete for the commercial supremacy it had held prior to the Revolution. It would have had a better chance had not destiny been so cruel to Aaron Lopez, who had done so much to make Newport the great commercial center it was. When things settled down after the British departure and it looked brighter and more promising, Lopez was once again ready to take up his residence in his beloved city, Newport, which gave him a haven from his refuge from the clutches of the Inquisition. On May 28, 1782, Mr. Lopez and his family started out from Leicester towards Providence in carriages, he himself riding in a gig drawn by one horse. In passing Scott's Pond in Smithfield, he drove the horse to the pond to be watered and was accidentally drowned while his unhappy family looked on and were unable to come to his rescue. Stiles recorded this fatality very sympathetically.

> On the 28th of May died that amiable, benevolent, most hospitable and very respectable Gentleman Mr. Aaron Lopez...He was a Merchant of the first Eminence; for Honor & Extent of Commerce probably surpassed by no Mrcht in America. He did Business with the greatest Ease & Clearness—always carried about a Sweetness of Behavior a calm Urbanity an agreeable & unaffected Politeness of manners. Without a single Enemy & the most universally beloved by an extensive Acquaintance of any man I ever Knew. His Beneficence to his Fam^y Connexions, to his Nation, and to the World is almost without a Parallel."

The funeral took place May 30th from the synagogue which Mr. Lopez had helped to build. It attracted the entire city. The Reverend Doctor James Manning, president of Brown University, delivered the eulogy. He took for his text part of the eighth verse of the eighth chapter of Ecclesiastes: "There is no man that hath power over the wind to retain the wind; neither hath he power over the day of death; there is no discharge in war." After enumerating Lopez's contributions to the community, and portraying in scholarly manner the ethical and good life of the deceased, alluding pathetically to the great misfortune of Lopez's drowning, President Manning concluded: "Mr. Lopez was a man of eminent probity and benevolence. His bounty was widely diffused, and not confined to creed or sect."

The death of Aaron Lopez was reverently eulogized in a poem by an eleven year old girl at the time, in words simple but effective:

ON THE DEATH OF MR. AARON LOPEZ

Awake oh heavenly muse, and guide my pen
  To write the Character, of the best of Men.
Who on the prime of life, was called to by Death
  By Heaven decree, to resign his vital breath.
He was a man, who was revered by all
  No one that knew him, but bemoan'd his fall.
Why say I fall, for if Bliss to Virtue is given
  Sure his is rewarded, in high of Heaven.
He was a friend, and father to the poor,
  But they alas, can call on him, no more.
In all transactions he was just and fair,
  Oh there is few left, that could with him compare.
He loved his God and his Religion prized
  And in each point was virtuous and concise.
He loved his parents, Children and his Wife,
  And thought them, the greatest Blessings in his
    life.
Then what must their anguish & their sorrow be,
  Since they no more, the best of men can see.
Oh gracious heaven, through your extensive power,
  Sooth and console them, in this painful hour.
And with your bounteous hand, send quick relief,
  To cease their pain, and alleviate their grief.
More would I say, but it's past my Art
  To paint each virtue, of his noble Noble heart.

These tributes paid to Lopez by Dr. Stiles, Dr. Manning, and an eleven year old Christian girl, reveal the high esteem in which all had held this noble Jew, who escaped the clutches of the Inquisi-

tion to come to this free State to be able to practice freely the faith of his fathers. Thus died the
man who laid the first corner-stone of the synagogue
in Newport. In his death the Jewish Community of
Newport lost one of its most influential members,
and the city of Newport, one of its most beneficent
citizens.

The tribute paid to Lopez by the local newspaper
lamenting his death was well deserved:

> That there is a Kind of Veneration which may be
> stiled natural due to the character of those most
> exalted for the practice of Virtue, appears from
> hence, that in all ages and in all Countries this
> Honour has prevailed—It is a Ray of Caelestial
> Origin, coeval with Society, and of so laudable a
> Nature, as to be sanctified to us by examples of the
> best and wisest Nations. A Tribute justly due to the
> Memory of that Man, whose aggregate Services ex-
> hibit in one point of View the most amiable Perfec-
> tions and Cardinal Virtues that can adorn the human
> Soul. That this is not inapplicable to the wellknown
> Character of this most invaluable Man, the Feelings
> of Hundreds of different Families will readily wit-
> ness, to whose Munifecence, Generosity, Benevo-
> lence, and Humanity they were recently indebted.

A document dated December 5, 1786 preserved
among the manuscripts in the Library of Congress,
speaks of Lopez as "an eminent Jew merchant, who
bore a most respectable, unblemished character and
was universally esteemed."

The unexpected and sudden death of Mr. Lopez

amid the unsettled conditions of the government
and business, coupled with the inflated currency, so
seriously reduced the assets of his estate, that it was
declared insolvent.

At the meeting of the Town Council of Newport,
held on October 14, 1782, letters of administration
of his estate were given to Joseph Lopez, Aaron's
son. Mrs. Sarah Lopez, the wife of Aaron, re-
nounced her right in favor of her son. The Probate
Court Records of Newport show that his personal
estate showed a debit of £3967. 14s. 10d. and a
credit of £1010. 19s. 3d.

The records of the Probate Court at Worcester,
Massachusetts, show that Abraham Mendes, Joseph
Lopez and Moses Lopez were there appointed administrators of the estate of Aaron Lopez after his
death under a bond of £5000. The administrators
did not plead bankruptcy, to which they had a legal
right, but conducted the business of the estate for
the benefit of the creditors. Partial payments were
made from time to time from the realization of
money through the sale of parts of the property.

On May 16, 1795, the house, wharf and stores
on Thames Street in Newport were sold for
$3800.00. Other real estate property in Newport
and Portsmouth was sold at the same time bringing a total $4908.00 all of which went to satisfy the
creditors.

An interesting item of the accounting is the sale
of a note for 14,473 Continental dollars against the

estate of one Joseph de Pass, which brought £3. 7s. 4d. No doubt this reduction of the value of the dollar and the value of real estate as well as rental after the close of the Revolution had a great deal to do with the reduction of the wealth of Aaron Lopez and the state of affairs of his estate after his demise.

A receipt from the Probate Office at Worcester dated May 18, 1795, states that Joseph Lopez "has made a complete settlement of the estate of the deceased . . . and has fully accounted for the whole of said estate so far as it has come into his hands the same being insolvent."

His son Joseph assumed to the best of his ability the debts left by his father. As late as August 6, 1804, a receipt shows his payment of such a debt to a creditor.

It was, however, destined that an eternal memorial should be left to testify to Aaron Lopez's generosity and life. His residence in Leicester and the estate around it which belonged to him were converted into a scholastic institution known to this day as "The Leicester Academy." The Academy has since become the alma mater of many of the foremost men of America.

To mark the resting place of Aaron Lopez his family caused the erection of a memorial stone in the old Jewish cemetery in Newport. It bears an inscription in Hebrew and in English.

The Hebrew reads:

A good name is better than precious ointment, and
the day of death is better than the day of birth

Hear the voice of Aaron

The Monument
of the burial place of the honored Mr. Aaron Lopez
who was liberated for Paradise on the 14th day of
the month Sivan in the year 5542.
    May his soul be bound up in the bands of life.

The English reads:

In Memory of Mr. Aaron Lopez
who was drawn from this Transitory existence
to Eternal rest, the 14th of Sivan A.M. 5542.
Corresponding to May 28th, 1782.
AEtatis 51

He was a Merchant of Eminence
of Polite & amiable manners
Hospitality, Liberality and
Benevolence were his true
Characteristicks an ornament
and valuable Pillar to the Jewish
Society of which he was a
Member, his knowledge in
Commerce was unbounded
and his integrity irreproachable
thus he lived & Died much
regretteed, esteemed & loved by all.

At the bottom of the memorial the Hebrew phrase
was inscribed:

"THE MEMORY OF THE JUST IS BLESSED"

JUDAH TOURO

JUDAH TOURO

JUDAH TOURO

THE ANNALS of the American Past are replete with names of Spanish-Portuguese Jews who have lived in and worked for the New World. Some accompanied Columbus on his heroic journey. Some Spanish-Portuguese Jews are found among the original settlers of certain American communities; others were among the earliest immigrants to the already existing colonies. Some are found with other colonists, fighting heroically on the battlefields for independence; and others, at home, assisting the cause of the American Revolution. Some stand out as great merchants; others as efficient manufacturers. But, from among all the early Spanish-Portuguese Jewish settlers in America who became famous in one way or another, the name of Touro is most outstanding and best known.

The one who made the name of Touro renowned was Judah Touro. He belonged to an old Spanish family which in its native land bore the name "Toro." Persecution, inquisition and massacre dispersed the Toros of Spain from their native land.

Through the Netherlands and the West Indies—
havens of refuge for the expelled and down-trodden
of Spain and Portugal—they found their way to
North America. In the course of their wanderings
the name became "Touro".

The Touros produced a number of prominent
men. It seems that for a long time the family cen-
tered about Amsterdam, in the Netherlands, where
many of its members occupied important positions
in Jewish community life. The records of the Se-
phardic community of Amsterdam contain frequent
reference to the name of Touro.

In 1664 one Abraham, the son of Judah Touro
was "Gabai de Terra Santa"—chairman of the
charities for the Holy Land—of the Spanish-Portuguese Jewish community of Amsterdam. Twenty
years later, in 1684, he was president of the Congregation. In 1716, one of three sons of this Abraham, whom the records record as "Is", which un-
doubtedly stands for Isaac, was president of the
Congregation. Another son, Joseph, was adminis-
trator of the clothing for the poor scholars in the
year 1702. In 1706 he was president of the society
"Bikur Holim", dedicated to visiting and care of
the sick. Joseph was also president of the Talmud
Torah in 1711 and treasurer of the society Bikur
Holim in 1732.

A third son of this Abraham Touro, Moseh, occupied the position of chairman of the charities for
the Holy Land in 1707, and of president of the
society for the visiting and care of the sick in 1710.

In 1683, towards the end of the seventeenth century, there flourished in Amsterdam a great scholar and Bible exegete, whose name comes down in the records as "Juda Touro". This Juda was very likely the father of Abraham who was interested in Palestine charities. In the beginning of the eighteenth century we find in the same city a distinguished philanthropist by the name of Manuel Touro. He expended money freely for all charitable purposes and may be the same as the "Moseh" Touro, the son of Abraham, who was both chairman of the Palestine charities and president of the society for visiting the sick. That the same person should be known by two different names, one in Hebrew as recorded in the synagogue records and one used outside of the synagogue is nothing unusual.

The similarity between the given names of the Touros in Holland and those in America is very noticeable. The periodic recurrence of such names as Isaac, Judah, and Abraham is striking, and suggests the direct descent of the American Touros from those in the Netherlands.

There is but one connection still missing in tracing the genealogy of Judah Touro back to the "Juda Touro", the Bible exegete, who flourished in Amsterdam, towards the end of the seventeenth century.

The first member of the Touro family destined to become a part of the "noblesse" of Spanish-Portuguese Jewry in America was the Reverend Isaac de Abraham Touro. Whether Reverend Mr. Touro came directly to Newport from Holland or arrived from the West Indies, which were Dutch colonies, cannot be ascertained with certainty. He is referred to in a contemporary record as a "Hazan from Amsterdam", which may be taken as evidence that he came to North America directly from Amsterdam, where he was born and studied for the ministry.

A very romantic tale has been woven around the story of the coming of Isaac Touro to Newport.

It was in the middle of the eighteenth century. Isaac Touro was attending the Rabbinical Academy in Amsterdam, living there together with his sister. It was a common thing in those days for captains of ships sailing the high seas to kidnap young men to make them members of their crews. It was diffi· cult to obtain sailors in those days, for the occupation was dangerous—often requiring sailing the stormy seas for weeks and months without seeing land or light.

Late one afternoon when Isaac was taking a walk to relax from both his studies and his worries about a member of the family imprisoned by the Holy Inquisition in Spain, he was approached by an unknown man who asked him to accompany him to render some assistance to someone in trouble. Isaac, being by nature a good-hearted person, easily fell into this snare. He accompanied the stranger and never returned to the Academy. He had been seized and given over to the captain of a boat which immediately put to sea towards the shores of the New World.

On the boat Isaac was forced to endure many hardships, one of which was on account of his refusal to eat anything except fruit and vegetables because of his strict observance of Jewish dietary laws. By chance he made the acquaintance of Dr. Ezra Stiles, the famous student of Hebrew and later president of Yale University, who was returning on that boat to Newport. Through the influence of Stiles who recognized in Isaac Touro great wisdom and scholarship, the captain of the boat changed his attitude and extended Touro many favors together with the promise to allow him to be redeemed by the flourishing and growing Jewish community of Newport of which he had been informed by Dr. Stiles. Dr. Stiles promised Touro that as soon as he landed he would inform his Jewish friends and effect his release. However, the accumulated ministerial duties of Dr. Stiles, who was the Congregational minister in Newport, were so pressing that as he landed in Newport he forgot about Isaac Touro.

Isaac would have remained on the boat as a forced laborer, for the boat was soon to set sail again, had it not been for the daughter of Judah Hays, Reyna. She, who had come to the harbor to meet the boat, noticed Isaac and fell in love with him on first sight. Through her father, Isaac Touro was finally released.

This happened shortly before the celebration of
a Jewish festival. On the approach of the festival,
when the members of the Jewish community gathered in their synagogue which consisted of a large
rented room in a private house, Mr. Touro was
asked to conduct the services, having informed the
Congregation that he was capable and had been
ordained to do so. Following Mr. Touro's officiat-
ing for the first time, he was publicly proclaimed
as the spiritual leader of the Jewish community of
Newport.

So much for the story.

Documentary evidence is not extant as to the
exact date of the arrival of the Reverend Isaac
Touro in Newport. In 1760, he officiated at a wed-
ding in Newport. The year 1759, the year of the
laying of the cornerstones of the historic Newport
synagogue, may therefore be the correct date for
his settling in Newport.

Isaac was only twenty-three years old when he
accepted the pastorate of the Congregation Yeshuat
Israel, which at the time did not have a synagogue
building.

After Isaac Touro arrived in Newport, the spiritual life of the Jewish community was quickened.
It was no doubt due to his coming that the Congregation Yeshuat Israel began the erection of the
beautiful house of worship, which was destined to
become a shrine of American Israel and a landmark
in American history. It is a masterpiece of Colonial
architecture and has been a theme for poetic song.

When the synagogue was consecrated on December 2, 1763, it was no less the reputation of the minister than the interest of the event that attracted all the dignitaries of the non-Jewish community as guests and visitors, and invited the description of the ceremonies of the consecration in the Newport Mercury of December 5,:

> In the afternoon was the dedication of the new Synagogue in this Town. It began by a handsome procession in which was carried the Books of the Law to be deposited in the Ark. Several Portions of Scripture, and of their Service with a Prayer for the Royal Family were read and finely sung by the Priest and People. There were present many Gentlemen and Ladies. The Order and Decorum, the Harmony and Solemnity of the Music, together with a handsome assembly of People, in an Edifice the most perfect of the Temple kind in America, and splendidly illuminated, could not but raise in the Mind a faint Idea of the Majesty and Grandeur of the Ancient Jewish Worship mentioned in Scripture.

Reverend Isaac Touro was very popular in the community. He was active in many organizations and was a member of the Masonic Order. He was a fine singer and of extremely good character. He was famous for his hospitality and his house was open to all wayfarers. Among his friends he numbered many non-Jews, the most noted of whom was Dr. Ezra Stiles.

In an age when the fires of the Inquisition still burnt, when religious liberty was not acceptable to the average man, Isaac Touro the Rabbi and Ezra

Stiles the Christian Divine cultivated an enduring
friendship. They visited each other's homes, walked
together in the streets of the city, attended each
other's religious services, and discussed together the-
ological questions of mutual concern. The only time
Stiles ever dined with a Jew was in the house of
the Touros in the company of a visiting Rabbi.

Among the Jewish settlers in Newport before
the American Revolution was the Hays family. The
Hays family came to North America early in the
eighteenth century, settling in and around New York
City. They came from The Hague in the Netherlands where they resided for a period of time.

Of the six brothers who bore the Biblical names,
Jacob, Judah, Isaac, Solomon, Abraham and David,
Judah became naturalized in New York in 1729. In
1735, he is recorded as a Freeman in New York
City. This gave him a better opportunity to engage
extensively in commercial enterprises in which he
prospered. He was one of the earlier Jewish merchants who owned his own vessels which were engaged in the profitable West India trade. One of
his vessels was the famous privateer "The Duke
of Cumberland", a small craft of about 160 tons.
During the French and Indian War, "the Duke
of Cumberland", mounting sixteen guns and being
manned by a crew of fifty, was used together with
six other vessels, all owned by New York Jews, to
prey upon enemy commerce.

Judah Hays was an active member and supporter
of the Congregation Shearith Israel of New York,

as can be seen from the records of the Congregation. He was a generous contributor to all charities and causes and was by nature a very liberal minded man.

Newport's commercial progress induced him to settle in that city.

Of the children of Judah Hays the one who achieved most distinction was Moses Michael. Moses Michael, who was born in the New World in 1739, is best known as a leading figure among Jews in early Masonry in the United States. He was appointed Deputy Inspector General of Masonry for North America by Henry Andrew Francken, who had been commissioned by Stephen Morin of Paris, acting under the authority of Frederick II of Prussia, the Grand Master of Masons of Europe. Moses Michael Hays is prominently identified with the introduction into the United States of the "Ancient Accepted Scottish Rite" of Masonry. He received high distinctions in the Masonic Order being addressed as "The Most Illustrious Prince".

Moses Michael Hays was a successful businessman in New York, Newport and later in Boston. He was one of the founders of the "Massachusetts Bank" and his name was the first to be entered on the bank ledger as a depositor. In his early days he was actively interested in the affairs of the Shearith Israel Congregation in New York and held the office of president of the Congregation. Like his father he was a generous giver to all needy causes, a supporter of education and very much interested in civic affairs. His name appears on a list of benefactors of Harvard College and on the membership list of the Boston Marine Society. A description of Moses Michael Hays reads:

> He was truly "an Israelite in whom there was no guile," a man of broad and liberal culture, astute in business, sociable and friendly with all, of open-hearted and open-handed charity which his well-filled purse allowed him to extend to all who required fraternal aid, whether among Masons or otherwise. Such aid he extended in a truly Masonic spirit and in no intrusive manner.

On June 30, 1773, the Reverend Isaac Touro married Reyna Hays, a daughter of Judah and a sister of Moses Michael Hays. He was thirty-six years old and she thirty. Rabbi Isaac Karigal of Palestine, who at the time visited Newport officiated at the marriage ceremony.

Isaac and Reyna Touro were blessed with four children, three sons, Abraham, Judah and Nathan, and one daughter, Rebecca.

Judah was born on June 16, 1775.

The only pride Judah ever displayed, the only occasion on which this weakness ever overcame him, was when he referred to the fact that his entrance into the world, like that of royalty, was greeted by the thunder of artillery. It was the artillery that marked the battle of Bunker Hill, June 16-17, 1775. Thus his birth was contemporaneous with that of the United States, of which he was always a proud, worthy and patriotic son.

Born into a family of distinguished ancestry and
into an environment of culture and refinement permeated with a spirit of broadmindedness, liberality
and brotherhood, it is no wonder that Judah grew
up charitable and benevolent. His birthright was
the belief in the brotherhood of man. Ancestry and
environment were for Judah Touro the rich sources
of his spiritual, charitable and philanthropic activities.

Of his childhood days we know very little. Under
the spiritual guidance of his father, he commenced
a thorough and religious education. Unfortunately
his father's guidance was of short duration. Ill
health and the perils of war forced the family to
move about frequently.

At the outbreak of the Revolutionary war, the
city of Newport suffered considerably. Its commercial, cultural and social activities were frustrated
in view of developments and war entanglement.
With the disintegration of the general community,
the Jewish community naturally suffered. The population of the city began to diminish. When Newport was occupied by the British, there remained
just enough Jews to constitute a quorum for Synagogue services. The bulk of the Jewish community,
in a spirit of patriotism for the Colonial cause, took
up the "staves of wanderers" and left the city. The
Reverend Isaac Touro, who had not become naturalized during his stay in Newport, and was therefore
exempt from offering up a prayer on behalf of the
British king, remained in Newport with the rem-

nant of his Congregation, continuing to conduct services at the synagogue. In accordance with tradition, he even allowed the synagogue to be used as a hospital by the British, this being the safest and most substantial building in town for such a purpose.

By 1780, the Reverend Mr. Touro, resumed the traditional role of the Jew, by taking up his "wandering staff," and leaving Newport. Together with his wife and children, he removed to New York.

In New York, in the absence of the Reverend Gershom Mendes Seixas, who had gone to Philadelphia with the majority of the members of his Congregation who espoused the cause of the American Revolution, the Reverend Isaac Touro for a while became the Hazan—minister—of the Congregation Shearith Israel. It was here that his son Nathan was born.

The Reverend Mr. Touro did not stay in New York long. He left for Kingston, Jamaica, before the Reverend Mr. Seixas resumed his duties as minister. What caused his moving to Jamaica is unknown. Tradition has it that he sought a warmer climate in the West Indies because of his ill health. Shortly after his arrival in Jamaica, Reverend Mr. Touro breathed his last on January 8th, 1784, and was interred in the "Abode of Life" in Kingston, Jamaica. He was only forty-six.

At the time of the death of his father, Judah was but eight years old. Left without any resources at all, Mrs. Touro and her children were forced to re-

turn to the continent and take up shelter and protection in the home of her generous brother, Moses
Michael Hays, who at that time had made his per-
manent residence in Boston.

It goes without saying that Reyna and her children enjoyed the hospitality of her brother. Being
a rich man he provided well for his widowed sister
and her orphaned children. Being a man of culture
himself, Hays saw to it that his nephews and niece
receive the education customary at the time and be
raised with a good cultural background.

The environment in the Hays home was conducive
to good character and helped to mould the minds
of the young Touro children.

Unfortunately it was not destined that Reyna
Touro should enjoy the generosity of her brother
for a long time. Nor was she to live to see her sons
reach financial success and eminence. On the 28th
of September, 1787, she was "liberated for Paradise", at the early age of forty-four, and was
brought to her eternal resting place in the old Jewish cemetery of Newport.

The two boys Abraham and Judah Touro, having
shown inclination towards commerce, were brought
up by their uncle—who faithfully cared for the
children as if they were his own—on a business
career. He took them into his employ, "training
them by instruction and example to strict honesty,
punctuality, order, diligence and perseverance". Although Judah was a year younger than his brother,
one puts it:

He was fully his equal in knowledge and ability and surpassed him greatly in rapidity of decision, energy, and determination, wherefore his uncle intrusted him rather than the elder nephew with the difficult commissions. Judah seemed, too, to realize more fully than his brother the gravity and seriousness of life and he seldom joined the young people of their own age in their amusements and frolics, but found recreation rather in solitary wandering to the most silent places about quiet Boston.

Of the two boys Abraham was the stronger in physique and the better looking. Judah was much more reserved, less inclined for recreation, more serious minded and constantly absorbed in his work.

When twenty-three years old, Hays sent him as supercargo with a valuable shipment to the Mediterranean. This was in the year 1798 during the time when hostilities existed on the sea between France and the United States. The ship in which Judah Touro sailed became involved in a desperate conflict with a French privateer, and after a hard struggle emerged triumphantly and returned home safely after a prosperous voyage.

This event was made the occasion for the development of the entire plot of the semi-biographical novel, "Judah Touro", written by Moses Wasserman. The author makes Judah Touro master the French language and speak to Napoleon to free a political prisoner, who is a descendant of a family in Spain, who had at one time in the past saved the Touro family from the Spanish Inquisition. Touro does this because of a tradition that he had

received from his father. He wins the favor of
Napoleon by his wit, saves his unknown friend, and
falls in love with the friend's only daughter, whom
he brings to America. Here Judah's love for the
girl is thwarted by a number of events. As a consequence he leaves Boston, and finds a haven in New
Orleans, where he spends the rest of his life.

This romance is the mere fancy of the novelist.
Posterity is always anxious to incorporate romantic incidents, especially of love, in the biographies
of its heroes, even if it is necessary to invent them.

It would appear, however, that Judah while residing with his uncle formed a love attachment to
his cousin Catherine who was a year younger than
he. Catherine reciprocated his love, but her father
objected to their marriage on grounds of consan-
guineity—near relationship. The objection of Moses
Michael Hays to the marriage of his daughter to
Judah Touro has surprised many. Careful reflection, however, seems to justify his action. Remem-
bering that Judah's parents died in their forties, that
one of his brothers passed away in his youth, and
that Judah was not of strong physique, it is little
wonder that Catherine's father was apprehensive
that his daughter's marriage to her cousin could not
be a long and happy one, and even result in regretful
and unfortunate consequences.

It is noteworthy that neither Judah nor Catherine ever married, but remained single the rest of
their lives, cherishing the sweet memory of a youthful love which found its expression in deeds of good-

will and charity towards all. When they died, only sixteen days apart, each remembered the other, in their last testaments.

It might have been for the purpose of severing the relationship between his nephew and his daughter that Hays dismissed Judah Touro from his employ. After he was discharged from his employment, Judah found temporary shelter and care in Boston with a kind friend, William L. Stutson. Stutson, a fellow apprentice of Judah, was willing to share with him his own small home and means; but Judah apparently had no desire to remain in Boston. His mind was too much perturbed and the Boston environment only aggravated his unhappiness. He determined therefore to leave the city, and, in seeking his fortune elsewhere, he hoped to forget his unfortunate love affair.

In October 1801, Judah Touro set sail for New Orleans which was then in Spanish possession, and later in 1803, was to become French, ultimately going over to the United States with the Louisiana Purchase. He did so on the advice of many of his associates, and very likely in the expectation to make his fortune in the newly rising commercial city at the mouth of the Mississippi. He arrived in New Orleans in February 1802, after a long and tiresome voyage during which he suffered so much that he resolved never to ride on a boat again. It is interesting to note that, although supercargo on a voyage to the Mediterranean in his early age, and engaged in the shipping business later in life, Judah Touro kept his resolution steadfastly, and never even came on board his own vessels while visiting in the harbor.

New Orleans was a city of about eight thousand people at the time Judah landed there. Although it was a good trading center and offered many opportunities for commercial enterprises, especially for imported goods such as Judah handled, the evolution of the city was rather slow. Epidemics of cholera and yellow fever, pillaging by organized bands of pirates, which have been made the themes of screen plays, hindered its rapid progress. The geographical position of New Orleans was excellent. Its transfer from France to the United States, in the Louisiana Purchase, which at the time was considered a most unbusiness-like bargain and a mistake on the part of the purchasers, proved a great incentive to the city's growth and development.

Upon arrival in New Orleans, Judah Touro opened a small store on St. Louis Street near the river, where he began a growing and profitable trade. The first stock of his store was the cargo of the ship that brought him to the city and which was consigned to him. It consisted primarily of cheese, soap, candles, codfish, and like New England products. Every vessel from New England, especially from Boston, brought him new consignments. Knowing he was very prompt and exact in his business dealings, with a reputation for honesty and sincerity beyond reproach, the New England merchants sought the opportunity to consign cargo shipments to Judah Touro. Once the cargo reached him in New Orleans the consignors knew their interests were secure. Ship owners, very early recognizing the integrity of Judah, would send their ships to him as agent to collect freight money and to solicit for them return cargoes.

His business was very prosperous. He accumulated money which he invested in real estate and ships, all of which advanced in price very rapidly, and before long he had amassed a great fortune.

Memoirs of Boston days left with Judah a desire for solitude. Psychologically, he found in the rigor of his hermit-like life, which he began to lead the first day he set foot in New Orleans, a compensation for his disappointed love affair.

A characteristic trait of Judah was that throughout his lifetime he shunned the company of women. The following story is illustrative of this. A certain Captain MacRea occupied one of Mr. Touro's houses, which, Mrs. McRea unreasonably complained was in a dilapidated state. To several messages, which she sent to Touro, he lent no ear, knowing her complaints were unfounded. At last Mrs. MacRea, after learning of Touro's weakness, sent a note to him threatening that unless he fixed the house she would come *personally* to see him about it. In short order, a carload of workmen with tools and materials of all description arrived at the house, with directions from Mr. Touro to repair everything according to the orders of Mrs. MacRea.

In his solitude he never crossed the boundaries

of the city of New Orleans during his entire residence there, with the exception of 1815, when in
military service under Jackson.

In 1816, Judah Touro transferred his business address to 15 Charles Street which as late as 1917 was
commemorated with a tablet. For a while his business was located in Exchange Alley corner of Conti
Street. In 1840, the Christ (Episcopal) Church on
Canal and Bourbon Streets and Judah Touro's residence occupied adjoining buildings. For some reason he never slept above the ground floor, making
his living quarters downstairs. In his house there
was a wine closet with choice selections, though
Judah Touro generally abstained from drinking.

His business enterprises made him the sole owner
of a 255 ton brig called "Comet". He was also part
owner of the ships "Judah Touro", "R. D. Shepherd", "Peter Marcey", "Delta", and "Massachusetts".

Judah Touro's business extended into many of the
States of the Union and agents represented his commercial house in foreign capitals.

Judah Touro was an incessant worker. Always
the first to open his store and the last to close it.
His exclusive interest in his business affairs might
have left a suspicion that he was mercenary and
miserly. He early accumulated enough money to
retire and live for himself. But as one writer puts it:

His arduous labors to accumulate a fortune were not
for the mere gratification of having money, for there
was no miserly trait in him; but the possession of

means enabled him, what seemed his greatest pleasure, to relieve distress and misfortune about him.

When most men have accumulated a fortune, they change their mode of life. This was not so with Judah Touro. He continued in his business as before. He enlarged it gradually to accommodate the increase in the trade. He never indulged in wild speculation, nor did he turn aside from his regular line of business. He conducted his mercantile enterprises in strict honesty, worked hard, and was so regular in his attendance to the business, that the story goes, when Touro went to open his store, which he always did himself, the neighbors set their watches.

Throughout all the time of the city's economic struggles, recalls Rev. Mr. Clapp in his memoirs, Judah Touro:

> pursued the even tenor of his way, ever calm and self-possessed, and with his robes unstained. The poisonous breath of calumny never breathed upon his fair name as a merchant and upright business man. The most tempting opportunities of gain from the shattered fortune which were floating around, never caused him in a single instance to swerve from the path of the plain, straightforward, simple, unbending rectitude.

Many a song and many a novel have been written on the theme of friendship. Nothing moves the reader more than a story of loyal friendship manifested by a heroic character in a stirring narrative. Indeed a life without friendship is barren and a person without a friend is poor though he may possess riches. A true friend is the gift of God. Friendship, said Addison, "improves happiness, and abates misery, by doubling our joy, and dividing our grief". It "adds a brighter radiance to prosperity and lightens the burden of adversity", says another author.

Judah Touro found solace from his solitude and loneliness in a loyal and enduring friendship which compensated for much of his grief. Shortly after he came to New Orleans he made the acquaintance of two brothers, James H. and Rezin Davis Shepherd. They were two young Virginia gentlemen, who formerly were merchants in New England and had come down south to seek their fortune in new ventures.

The Shepherd brothers and Judah Touro formed an undying friendship which only death separated. To their friendship may well be applied the words of Proverbs: "There is a friend that sticketh closer than a brother". They lived together, shared each other's sorrow as well as joy and were willing to give up their lives for one another.

The true and loyal friendship between the Shepherds and Judah Touro is exemplified in a dramatic event in the early life of Judah Touro. This event in the life of Mr. Touro is associated with his patriotism for the United States. It occurred during the memorable defense of New Orleans by Andrew Jackson in 1814-1815, and is recorded by a contemporary author. Judah Touro enlisted as a common soldier and performed all such severe labors as were required of him. On January 1st, 1815, he volunteered his services to carry shot and shell from the powder magazine to Humphrey's Battery, the headquarters of the defense of the city. He engaged in this very dangerous task amidst a cloud of iron missiles. Many stout-hearted soldiers in the vicinity sought shelter in the bomb-proofs. The British cannonade was unable to stop Judah Touro from performing his duty. He knew no danger. While engaged in this perilous duty, he was struck on the thigh by a twelve-pound shot, which tore out a large mass of his flesh and produced a dangerous wound, leaving him unconscious on the battlefield.

At the same time when Judah Touro enrolled voluntarily in the army in the regiment of the Louisiana Militia, his friend Rezin D. Shepherd followed suit, and became attached to Captain Ogden's Horse Troop.

Fortune had it so, that Shepherd became the aide of Commodore Patterson, and was assisting him to erect his battery on the right bank of the river, in the defense of the city. While engaged in this task, Shepherd crossed the river to procure two masons to do some work on the Commodore's battery. This was on January 1st, 1815. The first person Shepherd saw on reaching the other side of the river told him of the condition of Touro. Upon this Shepherd forgot about his mission and rushed to the place where Touro was lying. It was near a wall of an old building, in the rear of Jackson's headquarters. Dr. Kerr, who was dressing Touro's wounds, shook his head, indicating that there was no hope for Touro. Shepherd, not discouraged by the doctor's opinion, procured a cart and brought Touro to the city.

On the way he kept him alive with brandy. He brought him to his house, and procured some devoted women, who had volunteered their services to help Jackson's wounded, to take care of him. Thus Touro was nursed back to health. It was not until late in the day that Shepherd was able to leave Touro and perform the important duty that had been confided to him. When he returned to Patterson's Battery, the Commodore was filled with anger at Shepherd's neglect of his military duty, but was soon appeased when the latter frankly exclaimed, "Commodore, you can hang or shoot me, and it will be all right; but my best friend needed my assistance, and nothing on earth could have induced me to neglect him."

Commodore Patterson appreciated the feeling of Shepherd for his friend, and thought no more about the neglect of duty.

Touro alluded to this event, and to his undying friendship with Shepherd in his will:

And as regards my other designated executor, say my dear, old, devoted friend, Rezin Davis Shepherd, to whom, under Divine Providence, I was greatly indebted for the preservation of my life when I was wounded on the 1st of January, 1815, I hereby appoint and institute him, the said Rezin Davis

Shepherd, after the payment of my particular legacies, and the debts of my succession, the universal
legatee of the rest and residue of my estate.

Judah always remembered the generosity of his
friends and forever remained loyal to their friendship. When W. L. Stutson, who befriended Judah
in Boston when he was discharged from his uncle's
employ, became old and ill and became dependent
on a relative, Judah Touro found out about it. Immediately he requested his business agent in Boston,
Mr. Supply Clap Thwig, to do everything necessary for Mr. Stutson. After fulfilling the desire
of Mr. Touro, Mr. Thwig wrote to him concerning
Mr. Stutson:

> I have expended for him about thirty dollars which
> will make him very comfortable at present; $1.50
> will pay his board, so that $50.00 in all will be suffi-
> cient for the winter.

Judah Touro helped his friend secretly for he
did not want the beneficiary to know the source of
his support, lest it may embarrass him. He ordered
his business agent in Boston to continue to take
care of Mr. Stutson and expend whatever money
necessary for his comfort without disclosing his
name. Not until 1853, when Mr. Stutson under
all circumstances insisted to know the name of his
benefactor did Judah Touro permit Supply Clap
Thwig to disclose his name. Subsequently Thwig
wrote to Touro:

> His (Stutson's) heart overflows with gratitude, that

he has found so kind a friend to solace him in his old age after such a life of turmoil and poverty.

Judah's support of Stutson continued throughout his lifetime. After Judah was "gathered to his fathers", Rezin D. Shepherd continued to care for Stutson until the latter died three years after Touro.

The sages in the Talmud teach that it is better to give a person financial assistance by lending him money rather than by giving him alms. Still better than lending is to help one by setting him up in business and making him self-supporting and self-sustaining. This Rabbinic teaching was the basis of the famous eight degrees of charity compiled by the great Jewish philosopher Maimonides in the twelfth century. Of these degrees of charity the highest in order are: (1) Aiding the beneficiary so as to become self-supporting, thus saving him the agony of being a recipient of charity. (2) To give charity so that neither the recipient nor the donor should know of one another, as for example if one donates to a public fund. (3) To give so that either the recipient knows not the donor, or the donor knows not the recipient. In all events Jewish law prescribes that the giving "should be gracious, cheerful, willing, sympathetic and consoling". A person should do good for its own sake and must do so in humility, and not with pride or arrogance so as to receive glory or demonstrative recognition of thanks.

Judah Touro exemplified these ethical traits of giving charity in the truest sense of the word.

Early in his career as a merchant in New Orleans Judah began his philanthropic and charitable activities with the only thought in mind to do good and be kind. His philanthropy increased with his wealth. His charitable gifts needed not to be solicited if he only found out the party in need. And because of his insistence to conceal his contributions we know little of most of them. We may gather somewhat of an idea of his charitable work from some of the records of the recipients.

In 1830, Judah Touro founded the first free Public Library in New Orleans. In 1833, when the Congregation Shearith Israel of New York, which had been assisted liberally by his brother Abraham, found its synagogue inadequate, they addressed a letter to Judah Touro for assistance. In the same year, on December 19th, Rebecca, the sister of Judah, who had become the wife of Joshua Lopez, one of the sons of Aaron, died. She left to her brother, the only remaining member of the Touro family, an estate appraised at eighty thousand dollars. Judah, who by that time was quite wealthy in his own right, refused to accept this legacy, and requested his friends in New York to distribute the money among various charitable institutions, as she would have done herself had she lived.

Some poor missionaries from the native Christians of Palestine, approached several rich men of New Orleans to help them raise funds to help them rebuild their church in Jerusalem, but their appeal was in vain. A frivolous gentleman, in derision, suggested that they turn to Mr. Touro. The missionaries applied to Mr. Touro for a contribution. They soon returned to thank that frivolous gentleman for directing them to "so liberal a Christian". Touro subscribed two hundred dollars to the cause.

A poor widow, with several children, when all her means were exhausted, was threatened by the landlord with ejection from her tenement. She called on Mr. Touro for assistance. He gave her a check and asked her to go to the bank at once to draw the money. At the bank she was astonished at the fact that the teller refused to honor the check. Whereupon she returned to Mr. Touro's store with a heavy heart, remarking in indignation, "It ill becomes a rich man to subject a poor widow to insult and mockery." Touro who apparently failed to grasp the reason of the woman's remark, apologized, "But, my dear woman, it is all I can give you today, it is all I can spare just now." "But the bank officer refuses to give me anything for it," answered the poor woman. "Oh, I see," said Touro, at last comprehending the situation, "I'll send my clerk with you to the bank and you will get the money." Little wonder the teller had hesitated to pay a check for fifteen hundred dollars to such a poor looking woman.

From his place of business, Judah Touro, once saw a poor debtor, ruined through intemperance, being led by the sheriff to prison for debt. As he had known him in better days, Mr. Touro stopped

him and spoke kindly to him. Then having found
out the sum for which he had been apprehended,
Touro promptly paid it, and secured his release. It
amounted to nine hundred dollars. Commenting on
this act to a friend, Mr. Touro remarked: "I do
not much expect that it will be of any benefit to the
individual himself, but I have performed the act
for the sake of his family."

One of the most interesting examples of the
generosity and liberality of Judah Touro is his work
in connection with the Unitarian Church of his city.
In 1822, the Unitarian Church of New Orleans,
the only one in the State, was in debt for forty-five
thousand dollars. The Reverend Mr. Theodore
Clapp was its minister. Though the State legislature permitted the minister and the officers of the
church to have a lottery for the purpose of raising
funds to wipe out the deficit, only twenty-five thousand dollars was raised, reducing the debt considerably, but still leaving an unfavorable balance which
threatened the existence of the house of worship.

The church was situated in a growing business
section, where property values increased daily, and
where many sought to acquire real estate for business. Though the popularity of the Reverend Mr.
Clapp, the minister, invited great consideration on
the part of the people for him and his house of
prayer, nevertheless, it was impossible to raise the
additional twenty-thousand dollars to save the
church building from the auctioneer's hammer.

Among the many that appeared at the sale was

Judah Touro. Overbidding every intended buyer, Mr. Touro offered the twenty thousand dollars for which the building was placed on the block and the three knocks of the auctioneer's hammer sounded selling the property to him.

Not a few grumbling words and derogatory remarks were uttered by those attending the sale against the Jew, who as they thought had bought the property to turn it into a business venture.

How utterly disappointed they must have been when Mr. Touro, after receiving the deed and keys to the property, immediately handed them over to the Reverend Mr. Clapp. The congregation was not prevented from worshipping in the church for even one Sunday.

It must be borne in mind that the sale of the church was unconditional, and there were no stipulations as to how the buyer was to dispose of the property. In view of the rising real estate values in that section, the purchase would certainly have made a profitable business enterprise for Judah Touro, had he turned the church into an office building with some stores. Yet he chose not to do this. He turned over the building for the use of the congregation for a house of worship as before—doing this against the advice of some of his acquaintances and friends—forfeiting the twenty thousand dollars he invested.

Little wonder then that Reverend Theodore Clapp recalled this event in the following words:

It was a time of great business depression in New Orleans, when Mr. Touro became proprietor of the church edifice and grounds. Many of the society fell in the preceding epidemic. Some who were most prominent had just settled with their creditors. The friends of the institution were few, feeble, impoverished, bankrupt and pushed to the very brink of ruin. A noble Israelite snatched them from the jaws of destruction. From that day down to its destruction by fire, he held it for their use, and incurred an additional expense of several thousand dollars for keep-it in repair. He might have torn the building down at the beginning, and reared on its side a block of stores, whose revenue by this time would have amounted to half a million of dollars at least. He was urged to do so on several occasions, and once replied to a gentleman who made a very liberal offer for the property, that there was not enough money in the world to buy it, and that if he could have his way, there should be a church on the spot to the end of time.

Clapp adds: "For about twenty-eight years, besides, he, Judah Touro, gave me in small sums, from time to time, Twenty-eight thousand dollars."

Later when this church edifice burned down, Judah Touro came to their aid once again. In the words of the Reverend Mr. Clapp: "In this emergency the aforesaid Hebrew came to our relief. He purchased a small Baptist chapel for us to worship in, free of charge, till he could put up a larger building for the use of the congregation."

The Jewish population in New Orleans grew from one representative in the beginning of the century to a large and flourishing Jewish community in the middle of the century. Judah Touro erected a synagogue, at a cost of about fifty thousand dollars. He also contributed the money for the establishment of an Infirmary. Later both of these acknowledged his benefaction by assuming his name.

Touro's love of all mankind was manifested by his attitude towards slavery. It was his practice to purchase slaves and free them. He emancipated the Negroes who waited on him in the house of his life-long friend Shepherd, and supplied them with means to establish themselves respectably in life. He never owned more than one slave, though in his business enterprises he would have been able to vastly increase his profits had he acquired slaves. Such an act would have been against his principles. He did buy one slave, but after he trained him for a business career, he gave him his freedom with a handsome sum of money to buy a business for himself. In this the freed man proved successful and lived comfortably and independently all his life.

Judah Touro was scientific in his acts of charity. He aimed to rehabilitate the beneficiary, rather than to give temporary relief. His bequests in his will are calculated to that effect. It may be noted here that Touro was very careful not to cause any inconvenience to those who received this aid.

Two weeks before his death, in making his last will, at the age of 79, he was careful to include a paragraph to this effect:

It is my wish and desire that the Institutions to which I have already alluded, in making this will, as

well as those to which, in the further course of making this will, I shall refer, shall not be disqualified
from inheriting my legacies, to them respectively
made, for reason of not being incorporated, and
therefore, not qualified to inherit by law; but, on the
contrary, I desire that the parties interested in such
institutions, and my executors, shall facilitate their
organization as soon after my decease as possible,
and thus render them duly eligible by law to inherit
in the premises, according to my wishes.

His mind was not impaired, even by age.

Judah Touro was very fond of the city of his
birth. He shared that feeling with the rest of his
family, who all requested, as a last wish, to be interred in the old Jewish cemetery at Newport. Judah
included this wish in the very beginning of his will.
He said: "I desire that my mortal remains be buried
in the Jewish Cemetery of Newport, Rhode Island,
as soon as practical after my decease." His love of
Newport had been exhibited at a much earlier date.
When a resident on Bellevue Avenue near the cemetery remarked to a friend of Touro, "that it would
be a commendable act on the part of Mr. Touro
were he to enclose the burial ground with a noble
wall of granite, as the then present brick wall was
in a decayed state", it did not take very long after
that before a beautiful granite wall replaced the
old brick one, at a price of twelve thousand dollars,
which was enormous at that time.

It was this act of Judah Touro which enabled
Longfellow to sing about the Newport cemetery:

Gone are the living, but the dead remain
   And not neglected; for a hand unseen,
Scattering its bounty, like a summer rain,
   Still keeps their graves and their remembrance
      green.

His gifts to Newport were not to the synagogue and the cemetery only. He bequeathed to the City of Newport ten thousand dollars to "be expended in the purchase and improvement of the property in said city, known as the 'Old Stone Mill', to be kept as a public park or promenade ground." He contributed to the Redwood Library—built by the same architect as the synagogue. When he was offered honorary membership in the library, he in the usual "Judah Touro manner," promptly replied on November 27, 1843:

> I have to acknowledge the receipt of your letter of the 17th. ult., conveying to me a vote of the Redwood Library and Athanaeum Company, admitting me as an honorary member of that Institution.
>
> I have long since declined honors of any kind from my fellowmen; but in this case, coming from the place of my birth, a place ever dear to me, I accept the honor of membership; with an assurance to you of my sincere wishes for the prosperity of the Redwood Library, and of the town of Newport.
>
> Sometimes since I learned from my friend R. D. Shephard, that the portico of the building of the Library was in a rather delapidated state.
>
> It was then my intention to have made a donation for the purpose of aiding in repairing it, and I now have much pleasure in fulfilling that intention, by

herewith annexing you a check on the Atlas Bank in Boston for one thousand dollars, which the Company will please receive and appropriate to that purpose or any other purpose they may deem most useful for the interest of the Library.

I have also been informed of the defective state of the sidewalk from the head of Touro Street to the Library; it would be pleasing to me to know that the same were put in good order, by having the sidewalks flagged and curbed, and the street graded. If the company will undertake to have it done in a plain substantial manner, I will with pleasure pay the cost, on being apprized of its amount.

I will be much obliged to you for not giving any publicity to the above communication, and remain,

Very respectfully your obedient servant,

J. Touro

In his will which distributed upwards of half a million dollars to charitable purposes, two thirds of the sum was contributed for non-Jewish institutions. He knew no difference of race or creed, though to his last he remained an ardent observer of the Jewish religion.

Reverend Mr. Clapp remarks: "Mr. Touro gave more to strangers than to his brethren. With generous profusion he scattered his favors broadcast over the wide field of humanity. He knew well that many of the recipients of his bounty hated the Hebrews, and would, if possible, sweep them into annihilation."

Judah Touro's philanthropy was not confined to this continent. He was one of the earliest Zionists. In his last will he stipulated

It being my earnest wish to co-operate with Sir
Moses Montifiore, of London, Great Britain, in endeavoring to ameliorate the condition of our unfortunate Jewish Brethren, in the Holy Land, and to
secure to them the inestimable privilege of worshipping the Almighty according to our religion, without
molestation, I, therefore, give and bequeath the sum
of fifty thousand dollars. . . .

To this day there are preserved in the suburbs
of Jerusalem, Palestine, houses built with the funds
of Judah Touro. They are now occupied by needy
and dependent Jewish families.

Together with Rezin D. Shepherd, Judah Touro
expended the sum of $206,000 for an Alm House
in New Orleans, which was the first of its kind to
be erected in this country.

As we read the will of Judah Touro and behold
the many bequests he made to Jewish and to non-
Jewish institutions we can not help but conclude
that his knowledge of these institutions implies that
many of them must have been the recipients of his
munificence during his lifetime as well.

Judge Walker of New Orleans, who knew Touro
personally, gave the following character sketch of
the man:

How little of the hero, or great man was there in the
simple, humble aspect of that timid, shrinking old
man, who was wont to glide so silently, and diffi-
dently, through the streets, with his hands behind
him, his eyes fixed on the pavement, and his homely
old face wrinkled with age but replete with expression of genial kindness and benevolence.

Another contemporary characterizes Touro thus:

This gentleman was the humblest man whom I have
ever been acquainted with. A person overmodest is
very seldom found, or rather is to be looked upon as
an anomaly in this proud, selfish world of ours. But
Mr. Touro was too sensitive on this subject. The
most delicate, deserved, and timely expressions of
esteem from particular, intimate friends and acquaintances, seemed to give him pain instead of
pleasure. I remember being in his company once,
when a friend proposed to read to him a paragraph
from a Boston newspaper, which spoke of his character in terms of eulogy. He refused to listen to the
perusal, and remarked, with apparently excited feel-
ings that He would thank them to change the subject of conversation.

It seemed that the more he gave the richer he
became. But he made sure that no publicity should
be given to his charitable gifts. Again, in the words
of Walker: "He deprived himself of all other lux-
uries in order to enjoy and gratify with keener rel-
ish, and greater intensity, his single passion, and
appetite, to do good to his fellow men. . . . His
only art and stealth were displayed in the conceal-
ment of his benefactions."

In spite of Mr. Touro's desire to have all his benefactions concealed, his name became famous for
his charitableness and philanthropy. Nationwide
recognition came to him because of a generous act
of patriotism in association with the Bunker Hill
monument. Mr. Amos Lawrence, a Boston merchant, had pledged himself to give ten thousand dol-

lars to complete the monument on Bunker Hill, the erection of which had been thwarted because of lack of funds, providing any other person could give a like sum. Judah Touro, reading of this by chance in a newspaper, immediately dispatched a check for ten thousand dollars to the committee with his compliments, asking them not to give the subject any publicity. The directors upon receipt of this noble donation resolved that they "receive the contribution of Mr. Touro with sentiments of deep and grateful respect, considering it as a testimonial of his regard for the principles and the content for which, and its successful issue, the monument is intended to commemorate, and his affectionate recollection of the friends of his youth, and the place of his early residence." Judah Touro had a sentimental attitude towards Bunker Hill, for, as will be recalled, he was born the day the Battle of Bunker Hill was fought.

Reverend Theodore Clapp records in connection with the publicity given to this gift:

Mr. Touro once said, in my hearing, that he would have revoked the donation given for completing the Bunker Hill Monument, on account of their publishing his name in the newspapers, contrary to his wishes, had it not been for the apprehension that his real motives would have been misunderstood and misrepresented.

On the occasion of the dedication of the monument in 1843, in the presence of President Tyler, and Daniel Webster, the generosity of Judah Touro was commemorated by the presiding officer in the toast which has since become famous.

Amos and Judah—venerated names
　　Patriarch and prophet, press their equal claims,
Like generous coursers, running neck and neck
　　Each aids the work by giving it a check,
Christian and Jew, they carry out one plan,
　　For though of different faith, each in heart a man.

G. W. Warren, in his history of the monument, gave the following appraisal of Touro's character: "He was one of the smallest of all classes, into which mankind can be divided, of men who accumulated wealth without ever doing a wrong, taking advantage, or making an enemy; who became rich without being avaricious; who deny themselves the comforts of life that they may acquire the means of promoting the comfort, and elevating the condition of their fellow man."

On the 13th of January, 1854, at 11 o'clock on a Wednesday night, the venerable philanthropist was gathered to his eternal rest at the age of seventy-nine, sixteen days after the death of his cousin Catherine in Richmond, Va. He died in New Orleans in his own home on Canal Street which was later named Touro Avenue in his honor. The New Orleans newspapers and pulpits paid just tribute to his virtues, much of which he would have objected to during his lifetime. A resident of New Orleans at the time remarks: "No man ever died in the city who was more universally regretted, or whose mem-

ory will be more gratefully preserved." The death
of Judah Touro was regretted not only in New Orleans, where he had resided over half a century, but
throughout the United States.

According to his will his mortal remains were
brought to Newport for interment, on June 6, of
the same year. When his body arrived in Newport
on the steamer "Empire City" it was conveyed to
the synagogue and placed before the Reading Desk
where the father of the deceased had stood as Hazan—minister—more than eighty years before.

On the coffin two candles burned until the funeral
service was over.

Among the Newport City Documents is to be
found the exact record of this funeral. It is the
work of an eye witness; let it speak for itself:

> The funeral of the late Judah Touro was solem-
> nized the same afternoon; the procession was the
> longest which has been seen here for many years.
> The streets were crowded with people, the stores all
> closed, and the bells tolled. About one hundred and
> fifty Jews were present from various parts of the
> country.
>
> The City Council assembled at the City Hall, and
> marched in procession to the Synagogue, the gallery
> of which was already densely crowded with ladies,
> and there were thousands on the street who could
> not gain admission. The coffin stood in front of the
> reading desk.
>
> Soon after the arrival of the City Government, the
> Rabbis and other Jews came in procession, the
> former taking seats in the desk. As soon as the Syn-

agogue was filled, the doors were closed, and thousands remained outside, until the ceremonies were concluded.

The services were conducted by the Rev. J. K. Guthein, of New Orleans in Hebrew and English. In this address, which was excellent, he paid eloquent tribute to the memory of the departed.

At the conclusion of the services, at the Synagogue, the procession was formed in the order:—Rabbis and Jews from abroad; City Marshal; Mayor; City Clerk; City Treasurer; Board of Aldermen; City Sargeant; President of Common Council; Common Council; Redwood Library Corporation; preceded by the President and Directors; Protective Company No. 5; Citizens and strangers.

It moved through the streets as previously announced, to the cemetery, where the remains were consigned to their native dust. The Rev. Mr. Leeser delivered a very appropriate and eloquent address. After the coffin was deposited in the grave, the Rev. Mr. Isaacs deposited upon it a quantity of earth which was brought from Jerusalem for the purpose, at the same time uttering a few appropriate remarks. Prayers were then offered at the graves of the members of the family.

As the procession of the funeral moved from the synagogue to the cemetery the bells of all the churches tolled and the places of business generally closed.

The day before the funeral, on June 5, 1854, the city officially resolved:

Whereas, the late Judah Touro, of New Orleans, by his munificent donations and bequests to this city and various institutions within its corporate limits, has warmly and particularly manifested his attachment to the

place of his nativity, and whereas the mortal remains of
the said Judah Touro will arrive here tomorrow morning for their final sepulchre—therefore—

Resolved, that the Executors of the said Judah Touro,
and such members of the Jewish faith as may accompany
his remains to the city, be, and they are, hereby invited
to become the guests of the city during their stay here.

And on September 5, 1854, Mayor William C.
Cozzens reported his success in purchasing the Old
Stone Mill, and the land surrounding it, with the
intention to convert it into a public park, to be named
Touro Park, in honor of Judah Touro. Thus was
fulfilled the bequest made in Judah Touro's will.

On this occasion the Mayor expressed his sentiments in the following words:—"I congratulate our
city upon this happy result, and trust that this beautiful site, with his hallowed associations, may be
enjoyed by the Citizens of Newport for ages to
come; and the name, and I hope, the statue of the
benevolent Israelite, by whose magnificent donation it has been principally achieved, may be forever
associated with it."

The Mayor's wish to have the statue of Judah
Touro in the park was never realized, though a
movement to that effect was once started. The last
resting place of Judah Touro, however, was marked
with a beautiful monument of Quincy granite, measuring 13.5 feet from the ground to the point of the
obelisk. This monument was erected by his never-
forgotten friend, R. D. Shepherd, who attended his
funeral, coming up from New Orleans for that pur-

pose. In the base of the monument which is six feet square, a copper box was deposited, containing the current newspapers of Newport, New York and Boston, a copy of his will, and a coin of the year. To this day the monument stands unimpaired of its original beauty and simplicity, unspoiled by the wear of time, and the exposure to the elements. It bears the inscription in English and in Hebrew:

To the Memory of
Judah Touro
Born Newport, R. I., June 16th, 1775,
Died New Orleans, La., Jan. 18, 1854
Interred here, June 6
The Last of his Name,
He inscribed it in the Book of
PHILANTHROPY
To be remembered forever.

The Hebrew may be translated:

To the Memory of
Judah, son of Isaac Touro
who departed for the world of eternity
on Thursday, the 19th of Tebeth, 614, minor notation
in the 79th year of the days of his life
And was interred on Tuesday, 10th., Sevan, 614, minor
notation
May his soul be bound in the bands of life.

By righteousness and integrity he collected his wealth
In Charity and for salvation he dispensed it.

With the death of Judah Touro, the last of his name passed away. Yet the name Touro has become immortal. His life was not marked with brilliant

achievements or striking incidents. His voice was
not heard out in the halls of Legislation, neither did
his name fill the columns of the newspapers of the
day. Yet when the Reverend Doctor Gutheim of
New Orleans eulogized the deceased Judah Touro
in the Newport synagogue, he spoke prophetically:

> Years will roll on, another generation will succeed
> us, many a name now shining in the meridian of its glory
> will be forgotten and unknown; yet the name and mem-
> ory of Judah Touro will ever live in the hearts of pos-
> terity. Through the length and breadth of this country,
> the name of this philanthropist will ever be coupled up
> with the beautiful words of Scripture—"The memory of
> the just will be for a blessing."—"The fruit of the just is
> a tree of life."

More than half a century after these words were
uttered, the Congregation Jeshuat Israel of Newport, erecting a Memorial Tablet to the memory
of its first minister Isaac Touro and his two sons
Abraham and Judah, inscribed upon it the words
of Scripture: 'The fruit of the just is a tree of life.'

Such a tree of life affording shade and shelter to
many a weary was planted by Judah Touro, as is
evidenced by the munificence of his bequests and the
expressive tributes at his funeral.

Said Dr. Gutheim:

> Full seventy-nine years have elapsed—two genera-
> tions have since passed away—when, within the pre-
> cincts of this town, Judah Touro was ushered into life.
> Like his ancestor Jacob, he took the pilgrim-staff in hand
> —from the north he traveled to the distant south; like
> the patriarch, the Lord was with him and prospered his

ways; like the patriarch, it was his last injunction, "When I shall sleep with my fathers, then carry me away and bury me in their burying place."

His charity, like his friendship, knew of neither sectional nor sectarian boundaries. The catholicity of the one was equaled by the constancy of the other. Modest and unpretending, meek and humble, even to a fault, he delighted in doing good in secret, and felt happy in the consciousness of being the unknown cause of happiness of others.

On the same occasion, Dr. Leeser said:

If you had seen him in his daily walks, you would not have suspected him to be the man of wealth and the honored protector of the poor, as he was: the exterior of our brother betrayed not the man within. But when he gave you his hand, when he expressed in his simple manner that you were welcome, you could not doubt his sincerity; you felt convinced that he was emphatically a man of truth, of sincere benevolence. And thus he lived for many years, unknown to the masses, but felt within the circle where his character could display itself without ostentation and obtrusiveness, at a period when but few of his faith were residents of the same city with him.

Referring to the synagogue built by Judah Touro, as a free gift, without solicitation, for the Congregation Dispersed of Judah, Rabbi Leeser continued:

If you have ever been present during the hours of worship, you may have observed a plainly-dressed old man, seated in a corner in the upper section of the synagogue, devoutly engaged in prayers, not throwing about his eyes to the right or to the left, but feeling, as far as a man might judge from the manner he exhibited, as an humble mortal in the presence of his Creator ; and all he ever received was the office of opening the ark where the testimony is deposited before the reading of the law.

When the will of Judah Touro was probated in New Orleans, it was found to contain bequests totaling a half million dollars, three hundred thousand of which were left to Christian institutions and the rest to Jewish.

The "rest and residue" of Judah Touro's estate which according to the will was bequeathed to Rezin Davis Shepherd, his life-long and faithful friend, and which amounted to thousands of dollars, Shepherd, too, distributed to Jewish and Christian charities.

Thus ended the epic of Judah Touro, the life of a Jewish merchant. Posterity remembers only the heroes who have benefited humanity without egoism or personal pride. His immortality was not gained by ruthless power or personal advertisement, but by virtue of noble living.

Read the epitaph on the tombstone:

BY RIGHTEOUSNESS AND INTEGRITY HE COLLECTED HIS WEALTH
IN CHARITY AND FOR SALVATION HE DISPENSED IT.

WILL OF JUDAH TOURO

·Be it known that on this sixth day of January, in the year of our Lord eighteen hundred and fifty-four, and of the independence of the United States of America the seventy-eighth, at a quarter before 10 o'clock a.m.

Before me, Thomas Layton, a Notary Public, in and for the city of New Orleans, aforesaid, duly commissioned and sworn, and in presence of Messrs. Jonathan Montgomery, Henry Shepherd, Jr. and George Washington Lee, competent witnesses, residing in said city, and hereto expressly required—

Personally appeared Mr. Judah Touro, of this city, merchant, whom I, the said Notary, and said witnesses, found sitting in a room at his residence, No. 128 Canal Street, sick of body, but sound in mind, memory, and judgment, as did appear to me, the said Notary, and to said witnesses. And the said Mr. Judah Touro requested me, the Notary, to receive his last will or testament, which he dictated to me, Notary, as follows, to wit, and in presence of said witnesses:

1. I declare that I have no forced heirs.

2. I desire that my mortal remains be buried in the Jewish Cemetery in Newport, Rhode Island, as soon as practicable after my decease.

3. I nominate and appoint my trusty and esteemed friends Rezin Davis Shepherd of Virginia, Aaron Keppell Josephs of New Orleans, Gershom Kursheedt of New Orleans, my testamentary executors, and the detainers of my estate,

making, however, the following distinction between my said executors, to wit: To the said Aaron Keppell Josephs, Gershom Kursheedt, and Pierre Andre Destrac Cazenave, I give and bequeath to each one separately the sum of ten thousand dollars, which legacies I intend respectively, not only as tokens of remembrance of those esteemed friends, but also as in consideration of all services they may have hitherto, rendered me, and in lieu of the commissions to which they would be entitled hereafter in the capacity of Testamentary Executors as aforesaid. And as regards my other designated executor, say my dear, old and devoted friend, Rezin Davis Shepherd, to whom, under Divine Providence, I was greatly indebted for the preservation of my life when I was wounded on the 1st of January, 1815, I hereby appoint and institute him, the said Rezin Davis Shepherd, after the payment of my particular legacies and the debts of my succession the universal legatee of the rest and residue of my estate, movable and immovable.

In case of the death, absence or inability to act of one or more of my said Executors, I hereby empower the remaining Executor or Executors to act in carrying out the provisions of this my last will; and in the event of the death or default, of any or more of my said Executors before my own demise; then and in that case, it is my intention that the heirs or legal representatives of those who may depart this life before my own death, shall inherit in their stead the legacies herein above respectively made to them.

4. I desire that all leases of my property and which may be in force at the time of my demise, shall be faithfully executed until the same shall have expired.

5. I desire that all the estate, real, personal and mixed, of which I may die possessed, shall be disposed of in the manner directed by this my last will or testament.

6. I give and bequeath to the Hebrew Congregation the "Dispersed of Judah" of the City of New Orleans, all that

certain property situated in Bourbon Street, immediately adjoining their Synagogue, being the present schoolhouse, and the residence of the said Mr. Gershom Kursheedt, the same purchased by me from the bank of Louisiana; and also the said Hebrew Congregation, the two adjoining brick houses purchased from the heirs of David Urquhart, the revenue of said property to be applied to the founding and support of the Hebrew school connected with said Congregation, as well as to the defraying of the salary of their Reader or Minister, said property to be conveyed accordingly by my said executors to said Congregation with all necessary restrictions.

7. I give and bequeath to found the Hebrew Hospital of New Orleans the entire property purchased for me, at the succession sale of the late C. Paulding, upon which property the building now known as the "Touro Infirmary" is situated; the said contemplated Hospital to be organized according to law, as a charitable institution for the relief of the indigent sick, by my executors and such other persons as they may associate with them conformable with the laws of Louisiana.

8. I give and bequeath to the Hebrew Benevolent Association of New Orleans five thousand dollars.

9. I give and bequeath to the Hebrew Congregation "Shangarai Chassed" of New Orleans five thousand dollars.

10. I give and bequeath to the Ladies' Benevolent Society of New Orleans, the sum of five thousand dollars.

11. I give and bequeath to the Hebrew Foreign Mission Society of New Orleans five thousand dollars.

12. I give and bequeath to the Orphans' Home Asylum of New Orleans the sum of five thousand dollars.

13. I give and bequeath to the Society for the relief of Destitute Orphan boys in the Fourth District, five thousand dollars.

14. I give and bequeath to the St. Armas Asylum for the relief of destitute females and children, the sum of five thousand dollars.

15. I give and bequeath to the New Orleans Female Orphan Asylum, at the corner of Camp and Prytania streets, five thousand dollars.

16. I give and bequeath to the St. Mary's Catholic Boys' Asylum, of which my old and esteemed friend Mr. Anthony Rasch is chairman of its Executive Committee, the sum of five thousand dollars.

17. I give and bequeath to the Milne Asylum of New Orleans, five thousand dollars.

18. I give and bequeath to the "Firemen's Charitable Association" of New Orleans, five thousand dollars.

19. I give and bequeath to the "Seamen's Home," in the First District of New Orleans, five thousand dollars.

20. I give and bequeath, for the purpose of establishing an "Alms House" in the City of New Orleans, and with a view of contributing as far as possible, to the prevention of Mendicity in said City, the sum of eighty thousand dollars, (say $80,000) and I desire that the "Alms House" thus contemplated shall be organized according to law; and further, it is my desire that after my executors shall have legally organized and established said contemplated Alms House and appointed proper persons to administer and control the direction of its affairs, then such persons legally so appointed and their successors, in office, conjointly with the Mayor of the City of New Orleans, and his successors in office, shall have the perpetual direction and control thereof.

21. I give and bequeath to the City of Newport, in the State of Rhode Island, the sum of Ten thousand dollars, on condition that the said sum be expended in the purchase and improvement of the property in said City, known

as the "Old Stone Mill," to be kept as a public park or promenade ground.

22. I give and bequeath to the "Redwood Library" of Newport aforesaid, for books and repairs, three thousand dollars.

23. I give and bequeath to the Hebrew Congregation "Ohabay Shalome" of Boston, Massachusetts, five thousand dollars.

24. I give and bequeath to the Hebrew Congregation of Hartford, Connecticut, five thousand dollars.

25. I give and bequeath to the Hebrew Congregation of New Haven, Connecticut, five thousand dollars.

26. I give and bequeath to the North American Relief Society, for the Indigent Jews of Jerusalem, Palestine, of the City and State of New York (Sir Moses Montefiore of London, their agent), ten thousand dollars.

27. It being my earnest wish to co-operate with the said Sir Moses Montefiore of London, Great Britain, in endeavoring to ameliorate the condition of our unfortunate Jewish Brethren, in the Holy Land, and to secure to them the inestimable privilege of worshipping the Almighty according to our religion, without molestation, I therefore give and bequeath the sum of fifty thousand dollars, to be paid by my Executors for said object, through the said Sir Moses Montefiore, in such manner as he may advise, as best calculated to promote the aforesaid objects; and in case of any legal or other difficulty or impediment in the way of carrying said bequest into effect, according to my intentions, then and in that case, I desire that the said sum of fifty thousand dollars be invested by my Executors in the foundation of a Society in the City of New Orleans, similar in its objects to the "North American Relief Society for the Indigent Jews of Jerusalem, Palestine, of the City of New York," to which I have before referred in this my last will.

28. It is my wish and desire that the Institutions to which I have already alluded in making this will, as well as those to which in the further course of making this will, I shall refer, shall not be disqualified from inheriting my legacies to them respectively made, for reason of not being incorporated, and thereby not qualified to inherit by law; but on the contrary, I desire that the parties interested in such institutions and my executors shall facilitate their organization as soon after my decease as possible, and thus render them duly qualified by law to inherit in the premises according to my wishes.

29. I give and bequeath to the Jews' Hospital Society of the City and State of New York twenty thousand dollars.

30. I give and bequeath to the Hebrew Benevolent Society "Meshibat Nafesh" of New York, five thousand dollars.

31. I give and bequeath to the Hebrew Benevolent Society "Gemilut Chased" of New York, five thousand dollars.

32. I give and bequeath to the "Talmud Torah" School Fund attached to the Hebrew Congregation "Shearith Israel," of the City of New York, and to said Congregation, thirteen thousand dollars.

33. I give and bequeath to the Educational Institute of the Hebrew Congregation "B'nai Jeshurun" of the City of New York, the sum of three thousand dollars.

34. I give and bequeath to the Hebrew Congregation "Shangarai Tefila," of New York, three thousand dollars.

35. I give and bequeath to the Ladies' Benevolent Society of the City of New York, the same of which Mrs. Richey Levy was a directress at the time of her death, and of which Mrs. I. B. Kursheedt was first directress in 1850, three thousand dollars.

36. I give and bequeath to the Female Hebrew Benevolent Society of Philadelphia (Miss Gratz, Secretary), three thousand dollars.

37. I give and bequeath to the Hebrew Education Society of Philadelphia, Pennsylvania, twenty thousand dollars.

38. I give to the United Hebrew Benevolent Society of Philadelphia, aforesaid, three thousand dollars.

39. I give and bequeath to the Hebrew Congregation "Ahabat Israel" of Fell's Point, Baltimore, three thousand dollars.

40. I give and bequeath to the Hebrew Congregation "Beth Shalome," of Richmond, Virginia, five thousand dollars.

41. I give and bequeath to the Hebrew Congregation "Shearith Israel," of Charleston, South Carolina, the sum of five thousand dollars.

42. I give and bequeath to the Hebrew Congregation "Shangarai Shamoyim," of Mobile, Alabama, two thousand dollars.

43. I give and bequeath to the Hebrew Congregation "Mikve Israel," of Savannah, Georgia, five thousand dollars.

44. I give and bequeath to the Hebrew Congregation of Montgomery, Alabama, two thousand dollars.

45. I give and bequeath to the Hebrew Congregation of Memphis, Tennessee, two thousand dollars.

46. I give and bequeath to the Hebrew Congregation "Adas Israel," of Louisville, Kentucky, three thousand dollars.

47. I give and bequeath to the Hebrew Congregation "Bnai Israel," of Cincinnati, Ohio, three thousand dollars.

48. I give and bequeath to the Hebrew School, "Talmud Yelodim," of Cincinnati, Ohio, five thousand dollars.

49. I give and bequeath to the Jews' Hospital of Cincinnati, Ohio, five thousand dollars.

50. I give and bequeath to the Hebrew Congregation, "Tifereth Israel," of Cleveland, Ohio, three thousand dollars.

51. I give and bequeath to the Hebrew Congregation, "Bnai El," of St. Louis, Missouri, three thousand dollars.

52. I give and bequeath to the Hebrew Congregation, "Beth El," of Buffalo, New York, three thousand dollars.

53. I give and bequeath to the Hebrew Congregation "Beth El," of Albany, New York, three thousand dollars.

54. I give and bequeath to the three following Institutions, named in the will of my greatly beloved brother, the late Abraham Touro, of Boston, the following sums:
First, to the Asylum of Orphan Boys, in Boston, Massachusetts, five thousand dollars.

Second: To the female Orphan Asylum of Boston aforesaid, five thousand dollars.

Third: And to the Massachusetts Female Hospital, ten thousand dollars.

55. I give and bequeath ten thousand dollars for the purpose of paying the salary of a Reader or Minister to officiate in the Jewish Synagogue of Newport, Rhode Island, and to endow the Ministry of the same, as well as to keep in repair and embellish the Jewish Cemetery in Newport aforesaid; the said amount to be appropriated and paid, or invested for that purpose in such manner as my executors may determine concurrently with the corporation of Newport aforesaid if necessary. And it is my wish and desire, that David Gould and Nathan H. Gould, sons of my esteemed friend the late Isaac Gould, Esq., of Newport aforesaid, should continue to oversee the improvements in said Cemetery and direct the same; and as a testimony of my regard and in consideration of services rendered by their said father, I give and bequeath the sum of two thousand dollars to be equally divided between them, the said David, and said Nathan H. Gould.

56. I give and bequeath the sum of five thousand dollars to Miss Catherine Hays, now of Richmond, Virginia, as

an expression of the kind remembrance in which that esteemed friend is held by me.

57. I give and bequeath to the Misses Catharine, Harriet and Julia Myers, the three daughters of Mr. Moses M. Myers, of Richmond, Virginia, the sum of seven thousand dollars, to be equally divided between them.

58. I give and bequeath the sum of seven thousand dollars to the surviving children of the late Samuel Myers, of Richmond, Virginia, to be equally divided between them in token of my remembrance.

59. I give and bequeath to my friend Mr. Supply Clapp Twing, of Boston, Mass., the sum of five thousand dollars, as a token of my esteem and kind remembrance.

60. I give and bequeath the sum of three thousand dollars to my friends the Rev. Moses N. Nathan, now of London, and his wife, to be equally divided between them.

61. I give and bequeath the sum of three thousand dollars to my respected friend the Rev. Isaac Leeser, of Philadelphia as a token of my regard.

62. I give and bequeath the sum of three thousand dollars to my friend the Rev. Theodore Clapp, of New Orleans, in token of my remembrance.

63. To Mistress Ellen Brooks, wife of Gorham Brooks, Esquire, of Boston, Mass., and daughter of my friend and executor Rezin Davis Shepherd, I give the sum of five thousand dollars, the same to be employed by my executors, in the purchase of a suitable memorial to her as an earnest of my very kind regard.

64. I give and bequeath the sum of twenty-five hundred dollars, to be employed by my executors in the purchase of a suitable memorial of my esteem, to be presented to Mrs. M. D. Josephs, wife of my friend, Aaron K. Josephs, Esq., of this city.

65. I give and bequeath the sum of twenty-five hundred dollars to be employed by my executors in the purchase of a suitable memorial of my esteem for Mistress Rebecca Kursheedt, wife of Mr. Benjamin Florance, of New Orleans.

66. I revoke all other wills or testaments, which I may have made previously to these presents.

Thus, it was, that this testament or last will was dictated to me, the notary, by the said testator, in presence of the witnesses herein above named, and undersigned, and I have written the same, such as it was dictated to me, by the testator, in my own proper hand, in presence of said witnesses; and having read this testament in a loud and audible voice to the said testator, in presence of said witnesses, he, the said testator, declared in the same presence, that he well understood the same and persisted therein.

All of which was done at one time without interruption or turning aside to other acts.

Thus done and passed at the said City of New Orleans, at the said residence of the said Mr. Judah Touro, the day, month and year first before written in the presence of Messrs. Jonathan Montgomery, Henry Shepherd, Jr., and George Washington Lee, all three being the witnesses as aforesaid, who, with the said testator, and me, the said notary, have hereunto signed their names.

(Signed,)
J. Touro,
J. Montgomery,
H. Shepherd, Jr.,
Geo. W. Lee,
Thos. Layton, Notary Public.

ADDRESS OF PRESIDENT GEORGE WASHINGTON

"To the Hebrew Congregation in Newport Rhode Island.

Gentlemen.

While I receive, with much satisfaction, your address replete with expressions of affection and esteem, I rejoice in the opportunity of assuring you, that I shall always retain a grateful remembrance of the cordial welcome I experienced in my visit to Newport, from all classes of Citizens.

The reflection on the days of difficulty and danger which are past is rendered the more sweet, from a consciousness that they are succeeded by days of uncommon prosperity and security. If we have wisdom to make the best use of the advantages with which we are now favored, we cannot fail, under the just administration of a goodly government, to become a great and a happy people.

The Citizens of the United States of America have a right to applaud themselves for having given to mankind examples of an enlarged and liberal policy: a policy worthy of imitation. All possess alike liberty of conscience and immunities of citizenship. It is now no more that toleration is spoken of, as if it was by the indulgence of one class of people, that another enjoyed the exercise of their inherent natural rights. For happily the Government of the United States, which gives to bigotry no sanction, to persecution no assistance requires only that they who live under its protection should demean themselves as good citizens, in giving it on all occasions their effectual support.

It would be inconsistent with the frankness of my character not to avow that I am pleased with your favorable opinion of my administration, and fervent wishes for my felicity. May the Children of the Stock of Abraham, who dwell in this land, continue to merit and enjoy the good will of the other Inhabitants, while every one shall sit in safety under his own vine and fig-tree, and there shall be none to make him afraid. May the father of all mercies scatter light and not darkness in our paths, and make us all in our several vocations useful here, and in his own due time and way everlastingly happy.

G. WASHINGTON"

To the Hebrew Congregation in Newport
Rhode Island.

Gentlemen

While I receive, with much satisfaction,
your Address replete with expressions of affection
and esteem; I rejoice in the opportunity of assuring
you, that I shall always retain a grateful remem=
brance of the cordial welcome I experienced in
my visit to Newport, from all classes of Citizens.

The reflection on the days of difficulty and
danger which are past is rendered the more sweet,
from a consciousness that they are succeeded by days
of uncommon prosperity and security. If we have
wisdom to make the best use of the advantages with
which we are now favored, we cannot fail, under the
just administration of a good Government, to become
a great and a happy people.

The Citizens of the United States of America
have a right to applaud themselves for having given
to Mankind examples of an enlarged and liberal
policy: a policy worthy of imitation. All possess
alike liberty of conscience and immunities of
citizenship It is now no more that toleration is
spoken of, as if it was by the indulgence of one
class of people, that another enjoyed the exercise
of their inherent natural rights. For happily
                                        the

the Government of the United States, which gives to bigotry no sanction, to persecution no assistance, requires only that they who live under its protection should demean themselves as good citizens, in giving it on all occasions their effectual support.

      It would be inconsistent with the frankness of my character not to avow that I am pleased with your favorable opinion of my administration, and fervent wishes for my felicity. May the children of the Stock of Abraham, who dwell in this land, continue to merit and enjoy the good will of the other Inhabitants; while every one shall sit in safety under his own vine and figtree, and there shall be none to make him afraid. May the father of all mercies scatter light and not darkness in our paths, and make us all in our several vocations useful here, and in his own due time and way everlastingly happy.

        G.º Washington